Kim,

My favorite
VC!

It FqB!

I'M THERE
FOR YOU, BABY

The Entrepreneur's Guide
to the Galaxy

VOLUME 1

I'M THERE
FOR YOU, BABY

The Entrepreneur's Guide
to the Galaxy

VOLUME 1

NEIL SENTURIA

blackbird
VENTURES
LA JOLLA, CALIFORNIA

Published by Blackbird Ventures
2223 Avenida de la Playa
Suite 212
La Jolla, CA 92037
www.imthereforyoubaby.com
baby@imthereforyoubaby.com
(858) 754-3201

Publishing Consulting and Product Development: BookStudio, LLC,
www.bookstudiobooks.com

Book Design: John R. McCulley, McCulley Design Lab, www.mcculleydesign.com

Copyediting: Laurie Gibson

Wire Photo: © iStockphoto.com/lorenzo104

Author Photo: Brevin Blach

Library of Congress Preassigned Control Number: 2010917453
Publishers Cataloging in Publication Data

Senturia, Neil.

    I'm there for you, baby : the entrepreneur's guide to the galaxy / Neil
Senturia. -- La Jolla, Calif. : Blackbird Ventures, c2011.

        p. ; cm.

        ISBN: 978-0-9831704-2-6 (cloth) ; 978-0-9831704-0-2 (pbk.) ;
978-0-9831704-1-9 (ebook)
        Includes index.

        1. Entrepreneurship. 2. New business enterprises. 3. Success
in business. 4. Venture capital. 5. Senturia, Neil. I. Title.

HB615 .S46 2011   2010917453
658.4/21--dc22   1109

PRINTED IN KOREA

TO HYMAN, AUDREY, AND JANE

"Faithful are You in giving life to the dead.
Praised are You Adonai, Master of life and death."

—Jewish Prayer Book

CONTENTS

I'M THERE FOR YOU, BABY

After graduating from Tufts University 1967, I went to the University of Missouri in Columbia, to get a Master's degree in Journalism. My focus was photojournalism. I wanted to work for *Life* magazine.

As part of the program, you had to take some required courses. One was advertising. The other was news writing. I think it is fair to say that I did not excel at either of these courses.

In the case of advertising, the professor gave me a "D" the first semester. He suggested that my copy was reasonably clever, but that when I drew the ads I did not "stay within the lines." I suppose I was not very good at staying within the lines on anything. I argued with the professor that the concept of the ad was more important than the delineation, but to no avail. It was a "D" and a "D" it would stay. I was beginning to get a sense of my future.

In the case of news writing, I had a slightly different problem. I got a "D" the first semester in that course as well. I argued vociferously. I could see that there was a reasonable chance I would never get out of this dump, at least not with a degree.

I took the journalism professor for a cup of coffee and pleaded my case. His position was interesting. "You write well, Mr. Senturia, but you have no desire to stick with the facts of the story. You apparently make things up."

I looked at the professor and answered, "Sir, why would I let the facts get in the way of a good story?"

Whereupon he threw up his hands in deep dismay and laughed. There was no hope—he knew it, and so did I. He still gave me the "D," and I realized that my future was going to be more closely aligned with storytelling than with reporting.

I was not a total failure at Mizzou. I did finish third in the College Photographer of the Year contest. I could tell a story with my cameras, but that world of photojournalism was fast changing and rapidly declining. *Look* magazine closed in 1971 and *Life* magazine closed in 1972. The movie *Easy Rider* came out in 1969.

You didn't have to be a brain surgeon. "Go west, young man," said Horace Greeley.

Given my predilection for storytelling, where else could I maybe get paid for making things up? The only place where fantasy and reality regularly overlap is Hollywood. The movie business was beckoning.

So, after a year in the Army Reserves, I left the University of Missouri and went to New York University Film School to chase another half-baked dream (or scheme, depending on your point of view).

The reason I tell you the story about my adventures in journalism is that this book does not purport to be a totally factual reporting of reality. I am herewith, in advance, disclaiming any absolute truth to the stories that follow. They are close to the truth, most of the time, or at least some of the components of the stories are similar to what might have happened, or what I think may have happened—or given revisionist history, what should have happened.

It doesn't matter.

Rule #109: Never let the truth get in the way of a good story.

And to bastardize a great line from a great writer, Rod Serling, "That's the signpost up ahead. Your next stop, the entrepreneur's guide to the galaxy."

"THE, UH, STUFF THAT DREAMS ARE MADE OF"

(SAM SPADE, *THE MALTESE FALCON*)

Does the world really need another business book? And if it does, where the hell did you get this title?

I'm There for You, Baby: The Entrepreneur's Guide to the Galaxy takes its origin from my time in Hollywood in the 1970s.

Like many of my generation, I was drawn to the movies and to Los Angeles. Movies were the hot art form of that decade. Movies could move people from laughter to tears and back again. Movies could change the world. Think Lucas, Spielberg, and Coppola. They were the gods of my generation. And I wanted to make movies.

Today, the hottest form of media might be a 3-D, wrap-around, social media, five-square, GPS, location-based Twitter feed that you can access on your Oakley sunglasses while you are sipping a Mai Tai on a rooftop bar in West Hollywood, which you could not get up to anyway unless you knew somebody who knew somebody who had slept with the elevator gate keeper and who would look at you carefully, consider your clothing, your hair, your buzz, your wallet, and then maybe let you up to a place where you didn't really belong or know anybody, but where you would try to make small talk and meet an agent or an actress or a director and tell them about the script you have just finished and the deal you have under consideration, in turn-around, in pre-production, and just in case you are thinking of blowing by me and going on to the next pod of people who you might think are more important, I want you to know that I know the guy who parks Sean Penn's car at the Ivy. So, fuck you.

The guarded gates of Hollywood only open if you know somebody who is there for you, baby.

In 1971, I graduated from New York University Film School and was accepted as a Fellow at the American Film Institute in Beverly Hills. At the time, this was the most prestigious postgraduate film school in the country. They took 13 students that year. It was the second year of the school and there was no charge to attend. It was a real fellowship. I wasn't smart enough to be a Rhodes, but hey, I was an AFI Fellow.

Nota bene: One of the Fellows from the first year was David Lynch. He did *Eraserhead* at AFI and went on to a career that included four Academy Award nominations. In my year. there was a cinematographer by the name of Caleb Deschanel, who went on to be nominated for five Academy Awards. It was definitely the place to be.

The AFI flew me out for the interview. They paid the airfare. In my world this was unheard of. I will never forget my first interview. I landed at LAX and took a taxi to the Institute, located in a modest 55-room, 49,000-square-foot castle called the Greystone Mansion. Pinch me.

Greystone was built in 1928 and was a gift from Edward L. Doheny to his son, Edward "Ned" Doheny Jr. At the time it was the most expensive house ever built in California. Edward L. was in the oil business. He also happened to be the principal character in that charming scheme known as the Teapot Dome Scandal.

Rule #303: "Behind every great fortune lies a great crime." —Honore de Balzac

But, as you know, the wheel is always spinning. Four months after Ned moved in with his five children, he was involved in a murder-suicide with his secretary, Hugh Plunket—might have been murder, might have been suicide, no matter how you sliced it, it was Hollywood scandal at its best.

And that is where I was headed for the next two years. Up into Beverly Hills and the Doheny Estate and the Greystone Mansion—complete with a guard at the gatehouse to let you past the enormous iron gates. It felt like I had dropped in to visit Citizen Kane.

You gotta love America. I was on The Coast.

Hollywood held a special place in my heart ever since I was a young man in St. Louis and read the famous Budd Schulberg book, *What Makes Sammy Run?* This book is highly recommended reading, not only for would-be film directors but also for investment bankers, Wall Street traders, grifters, bank robbers, career politicians, insurance salesmen, real estate brokers, used car salesmen, gigolos, Ponzi promoters, and anyone else on the make, on the hustle, or on the run.

I loved Hollywood. I hated Hollywood.

How could one exist—let alone survive and ultimately triumph—in a universe populated by the following phrases that were supposed to pass for interpersonal communication and human connection?

"Let's do lunch."

"I'll get right back to you."

And the one that brings it all home, the granddaddy of them all:

"Hey, I'm there for you, baby."

In all three cases, you know you are getting fucked, and it will never happen.

Now you might ask, given my pejorative association with the phrase, why I picked it for the book.

It is because entrepreneurship is a little bit like Hollywood. I can teach the principles of entrepreneurship, but I cannot teach you to be an entrepreneur. The same is true in the movie business. There may be a map to the stars' homes, but there is no map to being a star. It is opaque, it is impossible, it is unlikely, it is different every time.

But somehow every year, great films get made and stars are born.

"I'm there for you, baby" is a reminder that the big con and the big lie are everywhere and that the pursuit of any goal is a singularly individual event. It can be done, it can be achieved. And it is worth doing. It happens every day in a thousand personal moments. Success, fame, fortune, and happiness. *Non problemas.* I am there for you, baby.

And finally, I hope that in these stories that I can vividly share the pains I felt, the rejections I suffered, the disappointments and failures I embraced, the successes I enjoyed, and most importantly, the lessons I learned. It has been a terrific run, so far.

Entrepreneurship is not something you abandon. It is like a permanent tattoo. For better or worse, you are a marked man.

What I always wanted was a mentor. I think there is no higher calling. To be a mentor carries with it a great obligation to serve well, to be the sherpa on another person's difficult journey, and to light the path but not to select the route. There are always multiple ways and there is no right way up the mountain.

Rule #161: When traveling in darkness, bring a flashlight—and extra batteries. It could take longer than you think.

I never had a true mentor, and so my path has at times been a bit more rocky than it might have needed to be. If I can shine a beacon on the process of entrepreneurship and Rational Man Behavior, then in some very small way, perhaps I can be your interim mentor. And maybe in our dealings together in this book, I truly, wholly, actually can be there for you, baby.

The "rules" in this book are designed to encourage, enlighten, and engage you in the ultimate pursuit of Rational Man Behavior. Whether you are running a multi-billion dollar company or you are the CEO of a company with three employees, every day you confront multiple opportunities to make decisions. Desperately seeking Rational Man Behavior takes effort and is a worthy goal that must be actively pursued. The rules apply whether you're in a small company, a large corporation, or a nonprofit. Today everyone has to think like an entrepreneur.

For example:

Rule #302: More money is lost through neurotic behavior than through bad business decisions.

There are countless examples, but here is just one from current events. Mark Hurd, the former CEO of Hewlett Packard, was having an inappropriate relationship with a female consultant, which resulted in his being fired as CEO, and the company's stock value dropping 12 percent in a week, a loss of more than $5 billion.

If you could sit down with Mr. Hurd over a cup of coffee, you might ask him the following question: *Just what the fuck were you thinking?* You put at risk your reputation, your wealth, your marriage, as well as the company and its 92,000 employees. What went through your mind, or even more importantly, *did anything cross your mind?* Or did you just assume that your actions were unique, inviolate, and protected from any consequences?

That kind of behavior is neurotic. It has nothing to do with computers, networks, products, outsourcing jobs overseas, 401(k) contributions, or anything else remotely related to HP and its well-being. It is dumb behavior and the end result of dumb behavior is always disaster.

In this book, we are going to try to help you limit your downside by giving you rules that might prove useful in your daily business interactions. The rules also demonstrate various principles and ways of thinking that might be helpful in achieving successful outcomes. You will notice that the rules are not presented in numerical order. The rules are the rules. Where they appear is situational and varies. I hope you will find that many of the rules apply not only to the "entrepreneurial issue at hand," but also can be applied to almost any situation in which Rational Man Behavior is the desired outcome.

Rule #261: It's not rocket science—it's brain surgery.

This rule applies directly to entrepreneurship and innovation. We assume that the puzzle being solved is a discrete packet, a concrete idea, e.g., how to put a rocket on the moon. But in fact, the problem being solved is how to think differently about how to put a rocket on the moon if you have never put a rocket on the moon before, and do not even know what a rocket should look like.

In other words, if it is about how to think differently, then indeed, it *is* brain surgery.

Innovation is about changing the way we think, it is about looking at not only our scientific or cultural past, but also our personal and emotional past—and finding out where they might intersect.

Rule #411: Try to enjoy the journey, because when you get there, the only thing left to do is check out.

CHAPTER 1

THE RULES ARE NOT MADE TO BE BROKEN

(LET REASON RULE)

Rule #1: Return every e-mail and every phone call.

The use of "every" can be modified within reason, but in general, adherence to this rule should be in the 90+ percent range.

There are several dozen reasons to adhere to Rule #1, and one of the most important is:

Rule #217: You don't know what you don't know.

The value of returning e-mails and phone calls has been well documented by hundreds of gurus, but people still neglect to do it.

Why? There is no good reason, period. It is a courtesy at the least, and at the best it may lead to a new and potentially valuable or lucrative or innovative piece of information. So, enough said, if you do not intend to follow Rule #1, at least in spirit, close the book, send me your name and address, and I will refund 100 percent of your purchase price.

CHAPTER 2

A GREAT DEAL IS LIKE A BOWL OF SPAGHETTI

(IT STARTS OUT COMPLETELY TANGLED, YOU END UP LICKING YOUR FINGERS, AND ALONG THE WAY YOU DRIP SAUCE ALL OVER YOUR SHIRT)

It was 1984 and I was working at Brookside Savings and Loan in West Los Angeles. I had a job as a junior dealmaker lending money to real estate promoters who were doing tax shelter acquisitions of apartment buildings.

The savings and loan industry was deregulated twice—once in 1980 with the Depository Institutions Deregulation and Monetary Control Act (with a name like that, you could make book that a disaster was looming) and again with the Garn-St. Germain Depository Institutions Act of 1982. These two acts allowed savings and loans to offer a wider array of products (history does repeat itself; witness the financial debacle of 2008) and was intended to allow savings and loans to "grow" out of their problems.

What it also allowed was a small gang of big-time promoters to gin up a real estate leverage machine that six years later took the industry down in a fireball of excess, crookery, thievery, misplaced incentives, and general skullduggery, malfeasance, and defeasance (a financing technique that essentially allowed you to book phantom profits years before they ever showed up).

And I got a chance to wade in this cesspool.

This was the era of the big-time real estate syndication machines such as Shearson, Lehman, and Craig Hall in Texas. The tax laws were favorable, and the money was flowing like the oil from the BP deep-water well.

The way real estate syndication worked back then was simple. You bought an apartment house on a seven capitalization rate, you made assumptions about the increase in rents, you borrowed 105 percent of the purchase price (after all, you needed to get fees), raised some equity to cover the negative cash flow in the early years (of course you needed to get more fees), you applied a fixed asset method of depreciation (the roof goes bad faster than the foundation—but then you accelerated all of it as if 90 percent of the building was going to collapse in five years), and finally you hoped like hell that the rents would rise before the whole house of cards came tumbling down, and that you could sell the dog to some dumb, unsuspecting, later-to-the-game syndicator who could do the whole thing all over again.

Is there any correlation between the big-time crookery of the early '80s in real estate and the big-time crookery in the financial world in the past couple of years? Think 2007–2009 and use the word "derivative" followed by "rating agency," then season lightly with subprime sauce and bake in a 350 degree oven labeled "greed is rampant." Can you spell musical chairs?

You gotta love America. Where else can we embrace an unfailing, inexorable, embedded in our DNA, permanent magic marker, blind willingness to believe that elephants can fly?

At any rate, I had a job and I liked it and I was good at it.

So, how did I get this job? Well, I operated on a simple principle. I was going broke and needed one. I was desperate for a real and steady paycheck; in other words, I needed a place to hide, just like the Bob Dylan song, "Gimme Shelter from the Storm."

Up until that time, I had been self-employed, having spent nine years in the Hollywood television writing racket as well as five years in the real estate brokerage syndication business (with some overlap since the charm of the starving writer passed into literary history after Hemingway left Paris).

Rule #107: Know your customer.

I was already selling to the pushers; I just needed a bigger stash.

And there was a young man, a very, very clever fellow named Michael Moers who was the CEO at Brookside Savings and Loan, and I had come looking for him to finance a deal I was doing—I was going to buy some apartments in Phoenix—and he assured me that he could "do that deal."

Rule #88: When you hear those magic words, "We can do that deal," bend over and grab your ankles. The corollary, "Done deal," requires a similar position.

"We can do the deal" is code for we will consider it, we will horse you around a while, we may do it, we may not do it, but we can assure you that if we do it, the terms will be more favorable to us than what we first tell you, and the closing will occur later than you need, and at the end of deal, you will wonder for a moment if the screwing you're getting is really worth the screwing you're getting.

Although every part of your heart and soul wants to believe that this time is different, that she really loves you, that as you look into her eyes, you know that all the other men mean nothing to her, that she strips because she needs the money for her two-year-old daughter, and she sends the money to her mother in Nebraska who lives on a farm that is being foreclosed on by the local and lecherous banker, and that pole from which she is hanging upside down defying the laws of gravity is nothing more than a tool of her trade, same as you use a computer, and that together the two of you can live happily ever after . . . And though everything in you wants to believe this—head for the door.

You can always come back after your erection has subsided.

But I needed the money and I needed the deal and so I said, "Yes, yes, yes—oh and by the way, what are the terms and conditions?" And Michael explained them to me. And then for some reason, in a moment of supreme confidence and I suspect to demonstrate the brilliance of his lending program as well, he pulled a massive spreadsheet out of a drawer and handed it to me. It was a

14"x17" piece of paper perforated for a dot matrix printer, and the page was covered —completely covered—with columns, rows, and numbers.

And frankly, I was mesmerized.

Now you need some history. The year was 1983 and the personal computer from IBM was launched in 1980 and I had bought one then and the first program I learned was Lotus 1-2-3. This is archaic by today's standards, but at that time, Lotus was very cool, and I was pretty good at it.

At any rate, there I was sitting in front of Mr. Michael Moers' large desk and all of a sudden, I was asking if I could come to work for him.

Michael is a fascinating character, and he will surface again later in the book. But his initial role was to make me a deal. Michael liked deals more than anything.

He handed me the spreadsheet and what he showed me was the numbers *but not the formulas*. This spreadsheet was the secret algorithm/financial model/black box that he used to make his loans. (He grew the savings and loan from $50 million in assets to $650 million in two years—a growth rate that that should tell you something about deregulation and the times we were living in.)

He said this was his holy grail, how he analyzed a deal, and at the very bottom on the right-hand side was a number in a box, e.g., 29.2 percent, and that was the number that showed the return on investment that Brookside would make if they did the deal. Oh, by the way, the borrower never saw this piece of paper. It was impossible for the borrower to see all the fishhooks because he was only focused on boating the fish—and Michael was intent on filleting it.

Brookside would offer terms to the various supplicants, running the numbers internally to see if the deal was good enough for Brookside. Then, using some fancy, arcane accounting rules, they would book the profit before they actually got it.

Stop. Have we heard this story recently? Can you spell Enron?

I love America. Only in America can you repeat the same crookery decade after decade and get away with it for a while and then when it is exposed, people say let's prevent that from happening again and then of course, it happens again.

Rule #74: The power and desire for financial innovation will always trump rules designed to mandate fairness, transparency, and equity.

But enough of GAAP accounting rules prior to 1984. Hail, hail rock and roll and just bow down to the wonder and glory of the spreadsheet.

Well, I wanted this job. And Michael made me a deal, and the deal was this:

If I could figure out the formulas so that when he input the numbers from any deal the result on my spreadsheet would be the same as the one he got using his spreadsheet, he would hire me. In other words, could I work backwards and figure out how the whole thing was assembled and how all the cells connected to and pulled from all the other cells?

Now this deal definitely had some hair on it—because all I had was the raw numbers from one deal, and I had to develop formulas that would work in all cases. You couldn't just make it work once from the existing numbers, you had to make it work generically all the time for any set of numbers.

(This wasn't solving the Google algorithm but it was not exactly a walk in the park either.)

This might have been a simple problem for a computer genius, but for me, a failed screenwriter with three-quarters of an MBA from UCLA night school, this was fairly daunting.

But I was good at math, I had a computer, and I was highly motivated. I needed the paycheck.

So I got up every day at 5 a.m. for three weeks and from 6–9 a.m. I worked on the puzzle and after that, I worked as a real estate broker: self-employed, hustling deals but without a lot of success. A one-man band with a tiny office.

After three weeks I thought I had it solved. I had written all the formulas and had regression-tested it with multiple data sets. It seemed to work, and so I made an appointment to deliver it to Michael.

I left it at the reception desk and went back to my one-room office and waited. He was a man of his word. He called back in two days and invited me into his office. I had gotten about 96 percent of it right. There were two tricks that I had not figured out.

Like the carny on the midway, he had neglected to mention that the milk bottles were nailed down, but still, he seemed impressed enough to offer me a job: $105,000 per year to be his junior mortgage deal guy. I was in fat city; I had found a mentor, not to mention that the year before my adjusted gross income was less than $42,000. So bring it on.

There is one other piece of the puzzle here. In 1982, I had gotten married to a wonderful woman who was a Wharton MBA with a wealthy father who frankly was not all that fond of me (the father, that is). And getting a job was going to make him a lot happier than he was in 1982, when he took his prospective son-in-law out to dinner at the Tadich Grill in San Francisco, sat across from me, played with his wine glass, looked at me with a puzzled frown and then, as if it were some 1950 movie, spoke.

"Young man, I have three daughters. One is married to a doctor; I know what a doctor is. The second one is married to a lawyer; I know what a lawyer is. And now you propose to marry my third daughter. You say you are an entrepreneur." (At this point, there is the pregnant pause that comes just before the tornado lifts Dorothy up into the black hole.) "Just what exactly is an entrepreneur and how do you propose to support my daughter in the fashion to which she should be accustomed?"

Rule #431: Happily ever after. Hah.

And so I became vice president of worldwide, strategic, global, wrap-around mortgage origination at Brookside Savings and Loan. I had finally graduated to the rank of Bad Ass—you want our money, you got to come through my door—you're asking yourself did he fire six shots or only five? Do you feel lucky, well do ya, punk? I had a command center desk area with three computers and a couple of phones. I was in full deal mode.

The syndicator would send me the "package" and then I ran the statistical models that lent crazy money to crazy borrowers doing crazy deals with crazy assumptions that eventually led the savings and loan into bankruptcy and put one of the two principals in jail.

Nice work.

I confess: I loved the deals and I loved the numbers and I loved the magic of the spreadsheet. Sometimes it was like trying to fit a 6-foot, 220-pound man into a 38 short double-breasted suit. It was a bit snug, but if you let out the back of the jacket, lengthened the pants, let out the seat, put some elastic in the waist band—well, hell, he may look like shit, but at least he could go out in public without being arrested for indecent exposure.

And the deal got done. Those magic words, "We can do this deal." Well, more often than not, they were coming true.

Now remember, the whole idea of a savings and loan is to lend money. We only made money if we lent money, so let's tell each other the truth. I was a salesman and my product was money.

And to be a good salesman, you have to be a good actor. And I had training. I had played the part of "the fireman" in Eugene Ionesco's *The Bald Soprano*. It was 1964, and I was at Tufts University, and it seemed to me that the best way to get laid was to hang out with the artsy crowd, and that crowd was resident at the Arena Theater. Ah, the theater. The greasepaint, the audience, the applause. Gimme a break. I was chasing a young Lady Macbeth and if that is what it took, well, I am there for you, baby. By the way, I did the play, got good reviews, did not forget my lines, and was successful with respect to the lady thespian I was tracking. All in all, not a bad semester.

So, slinging money for a living. Not a problem.

So the "fireman" went out on the hustings to tell the syndicators, developers, promoters, and hustlers of the world that we had money and round heels. Bring it on. Done deal!

I went to dozens of conferences where I would sit on the panel to discuss lending and what we were looking for and how Brookside did deals. Mostly what happened was I ended up hustling the other guys on the panel. It was incestuous, but there I was, hobnobbing with whales.

"How big a deal can you do?"

"Name it."

We figured once we got our hands on the deal, we could chop it up, syndicate it, tranche it, and get it done. Sort of like mortgage-backed securities, CDOs, CMOs, and the derivatives of Wall Street, 2007. Déjà vu all over again. Twenty-five years later and the endless loop of financial spawn has still never hit the pause button.

I knew my role. I was trained. I had been outside the tent, but now I knew the secret handshake.

I remember two years earlier, sitting in the audience at one of the Urban Land Institute real estate conferences—a hungry-for-a-loan beggar, hanging on every word, hoping for the banker on the podium to offer some magic concoction of asset class, loan-to-value ratio, and interest rate that would match my bingo card. Rapt, just listening to the famous big shots on the panel tell us the crap we already knew but hoping that it would be real for us this one time, that maybe they really would finance a mobile home park that was situated on a flood plain where all the trailers were inhabited by widows and orphans who could easily be displaced so that the rents could be raised, so we could flip this piece of shit to someone else—*who they could then re-finance again.*

You gotta love America.

And now here I was, sitting on the same panel at the same ULI conference, in a beautiful suit, in front of 400 fresh supplicants, slinging the same premeditated bullshit I was used to listening to, sometimes hedging my words but always, always ending with *"We can do that deal."*

And then I would bring home 30 business cards from the needy, and we would begin to troll for suckers to take our money because now that I knew the numbers, I mean hell, I did the numbers, I wrote the formulas, I was on the inside, you couldn't fool me—but for sure, we could fool them. And we did.

Michael made me crazy, but I loved that job. I could see the power of the deal in a way I had never seen it before. And I became a bit of an addict. There is no 12-step program to help you stop loving the numbers. I fired up the computers and input the data and out came that magic number at the bottom right side of the printout—and if that number were big enough, done deal!

This is the same magic carpet ride that turned Wall Street into a gambling casino 20 years later. After all it is just a game of musical chairs. You simply do not want to be the last man standing. Flip it, finance it, flip it again but don't fall in love with it and never hold it for more than the single moment it takes to hit "Send" and move the numbers to the next man standing.

I took pride in my work. I was drinking the Kool Aid. We were at the cutting edge of the real estate syndication game, and it is with some pride that I was part of the team that invented the first ever, not to be repeated, not even sure it totally worked "expandable wrap mortgage." This was an arcane device that Michael and I ginned up whereby we could keep lending more money inside the wrap-around mortgage as the rents increased, so that we could provide more leverage and at the same time lever up our assets. I became a student of defeasance. I had a blast. It was an early version of Liar's Poker, West Coast style.

"Return with us now to the thrilling days of yesteryear."

I am working at Brookside, and I get a message from an actor friend of mine, Bill Jordan. You can look up his film bio, but at that time, 1984, he was doing pretty well. He was handsome, single, employed, semi-famous, and had slept with every beautiful actress, model, or Playmate in town. I loved him.

And he says, I need to see you today. I told him I was busy . . . just jammed . . . and then he said, I *have* to see you today. That is when Rule #217 kicked in: You don't know what you don't know, so when a good friend implores, when he says it is really important—in other words, drop whatever the fuck you are doing and make time for me, goddamnit—then you have to go to lunch. Which we did.

We go to a Thai restaurant around the corner and he proceeds to tell me a preposterous tale of a real estate opportunity, of another friend who had a friend who had a cousin who knew people in San Diego, and if we moved quickly there was a deal to be had.

(This was before the Nigerian prince scam.)

Rule #188: Do not bullshit a bullshitter.

Frankly, the story was bizarre and made no sense at all but I had stood in the pulpit and if you are going to preach, you have to pray, and after all, ladies and gentlemen, step right up, there's a winner every time.

So Bill tells me that there is a piece of land in downtown San Diego and his friend (this is the friend of the friend syndrome) knows the skinny on the deal and is friends with the guy who is selling it and then he proceeds to tell me that it is across from what is going to be the new planned convention center and that it is in the redevelopment district and that it is zoned for a 500-foot high-rise condo. "But wait, there's more. If you buy one today, we will ship you another one absolutely free." This was the Ginsu knife of all real estate deals.

Rule #138: If it is such a good deal, why are you calling me?

Well, what the hell? I could see that my days at the savings and loan were going to end. After all, the government was getting religion, regulations were returning, the era of the rock-and-roll S&L was coming to a close. It would take a few years and a few indictments and a few trials and a few prison sentences and a few years of penance, remorse, and restitution, followed closely by the too little, too late RTC (Resolution Trust Corporation where, boy oh boy, did the pigs feed at that trough as well) before the whole thing would start again.

And what the fuck, I needed a new knife. So I got on a plane and flew to San Diego and went to see the land.

I spent two days in San Diego and talked to a bunch of land use lawyers, architects, brokers, deal guys, and of course that friend of a friend. And I decided I would buy it. I was a sucker for a good story, with a cast of colorful characters, incomplete data, little or no certainty about the future, or the who, what, when of this mythical convention center, but I had gone to the Moers school of deal making and I believed that if I could tie it up long enough, I could figure the damn thing out and maybe make 50 bucks.

Rule #39: You can either pick the terms or the price, but you can't pick both.

So I gave the guy his price, but the terms were quite favorable. It was $10,000 down on a purchase price of $1.8 million with six months' due diligence, followed by three additional six- month extensions with a couple of spin maneuvers and one triple toe loop. This land was tied up until the millennium. My buddy Bill was thrilled.

As time passed, the deal got more complicated, but it also got mo' better.

I started out with 30,000 square feet of dirt in the shape of an L, relatively unbuildable, and three years later I ended up with 92,000 square feet of land in the shape of a lovely triangle, in fact, yes it's true, across from the new, soon-to-be-built convention center.

And then **Rule #296:** So, what's in it for me?

Early in the adventure, long before success even vaguely loomed on the horizon, the actor and the friend of a friend wanted their cut. "Give us money, put us in the deal, we were there for you, baby, if it weren't for us, you'd still be picking your feet in Poughkeepsie."

Now the combined net worth of these two gentlemen was less than a ham sandwich, so in terms of their financial participation, it was not going to happen. But I did make what I thought was a decent offer. As time passed, their need for current cash superseded their 3.8374 percent back-end, subordinated ownership and at the end of the day, I paid them $100,000, and they were thrilled. Thrilled.

Rule #31: No good deed goes unpunished.

Yes. They were happy, until five years later, when I walked out with $3 million. But it is damn hard to look back and look forward and pay the rent all at the same time.

CHAPTER 3

NOBODY DOESN'T LIKE A TALL BUILDING

The twists and spins in finally assembling a 92,000-square-foot piece of land for a condominium high-rise are myriad. In 1975, the city of San Diego had formed a redevelopment agency known as CCDC (Centre City Development Corporation) to bring prosperity to downtown. Its first major project, completed in 1985, was a blockbuster success. Horton Plaza, an open-air mall brilliantly designed by Jon Jerde and built by the Hahn Company and covering six-and-a-half city blocks, stood the world of shopping malls on its head. It was a radical and innovative design, and it dramatically changed downtown San Diego. All of sudden the city was transformed from a sleepy Navy town with hookers on the corners to a world-class city ready for . . . downtown housing, high-rise condominiums, urban landscape, people, nightlife. Welcome to the big time.

CCDC was in full promotion mode. There were deals to be made, buildings to be built; the city fathers wanted a 24-hour downtown.

And there was lots of horse trading. To me, a movie guy, it seemed like Sergio Leone and Clint Eastwood were the mayor and the city council. For a few dollars more, you could build—and the folks at CCDC would lend you the shovel.

There were countless meetings and negotiations and, like any good Western, there was the ubiquitous poker game, and as befits that particular game of chance, there was a bit of, dare I say, betting, bluffing, posturing, and chip counting. One-eyed jacks were wild.

Rule #222: No-limit poker subjects you to the principle of being table-staked, which means the guy with the most money raises the pot until you have no more money to put in . . . and you have to leave the table. Not a good outcome.

Rule #283: "Pressure is playing for ten dollars when you don't have a dime in your pocket." —Lee Trevino

I had tied up this piece of property and now I needed some backers, some investors, some people with wild ambitions and a deep desire to make a lot of money. Enter my former boss, Mr. Moers, and his partner, Mr. Pastel, co-founders of Brookside Savings. This was early 1986 (I had left in mid-1985) and although the rules for savings and loans had changed, they were still doing deals—and keeping the federal regulators at bay.

So it seemed only reasonable to offer the two of them a piece of this crazy deal. After all, these were my former rock-and-roll partners; they were very smart real estate guys and they loved the action. Like the Blues Brothers, we would be bringing the band back together.

We would each put in a third of the money, but I was the one responsible for doing the grunting and grinding and I would get a modest fee ($2,000 per month), not enough to support my bride in the fashion to which her old man wanted her to become accustomed, but hey, I was in the game. I had a deal. I had upside. And I was going to see just how far I could take this baby.

Rule #40: Things are never what they seem . . . nor are the people involved with those things.

The only previous experience I had as a real estate developer was building a 24-unit, two-story garden apartment complex in Phoenix,

Arizona, and six single-family homes in Scottsdale, Arizona. So of course, it seemed perfectly reasonable to me that I should undertake the development of a 200-unit, 40-story condominium. Sure, I know that first step is always a doozy, but if you don't kill yourself, it is a hell of an E-ticket ride.

The first thing I did was assemble a team of architects, lawyers, lobbyists, and local big shots; after all, riding out of the sunset was a gunslinger from the north (Los Angeles) come to the fair city of San Diego, painting a picture of revitalization, of a tall building writ large on the skyline of downtown, promising that milk and honey would flow thereafter from its doorsteps and course through the rest of downtown, bringing with it further development and growth and tax increment revenue. (I had studied at the Elmer Gantry School of Architecture and Finance.)

Rule #398: Motivations are different for all players. Figure out who holds the most cards, find out what they want the most, and then offer to do exactly that.

The city wanted action—and action was what they were going to get.

"And oh, one more thing, please make sure this big building does not block the view of the bay, and if you could just meet these few (129) other demands, that would be great."

Rule #32: The screwing you're getting may not be worth the screwing you're getting.

The three caballeros each put up $100,000 (half my net worth at the time) and we began the process of getting the approvals. The date of our first meeting with CCDC was February 12, 1986.

It took two years of meetings, community groups, architectural review, hearings, opinions, problems, constituencies that needed to be heard from, and multiple trips to the city council where we could practice genuflecting until we finally got a signed Negotiating Agreement. The negotiating agreement is the precursor to the DDA, the Disposition and Development Agreement, which is the legal document that actually lets you build the damn thing. We were in the game.

Rule #183: The people who have the least money in the deal are usually the same people who have the strongest opinions about what they want you to do with your money.

These things called community hearings, community groups, community planning—they sound nice in principle. It is inclusive and people are entitled to be heard but being listened to is different than being extorted. The saga of developers and community groups is another book; I will not write it, but there are 23,459 of my brethren in the real estate racket who might have a few choice words to add on that subject.

At any rate, we finally get to the summer of 1988. My partners and I have now invested $758,000 and I am up to my eyeballs in debt and we have stalled the city and CCDC for almost eight months in an effort to hang on to our rights, which were finally beginning to look like they might be worth something.

Rule #299: Don't tell me about lemons and lemonade. Just give me a Hendricks martini straight up.

Stalling is an ancient financing technique, first used during the Roman Empire, when Augustus the Second was trying to get a permit to add a second bathroom to his villa and the Druids wouldn't let him out of plan check because he couldn't pay the school fees.

The more contemporary version of the stall was employed by yours truly. Keep dancing and don't let them see you sweat. Our exclusive negotiating agreement gave us set time frames to perform certain things—you need to do schematic drawings, identify funding, select a contractor, etc. In other words, you need to look like you actually know what you are doing, that you are proceeding to do that which you have convinced them you know how to do, and that you fully intend to actually build this thing for which you just spent the last 24 months working the system to get the approvals.

On the one hand, I am telling the city that I am there for them, baby, *non problemas*, we are right there, close to greatness, ready to go, waving our arms, just need a few more little details ironed out—and the rest of my days (and nights) are spent 24/7 scrambling all over the globe trying to find someone who actually has real money and who is crazy enough to want to build a high rise in downtown San Diego, where prior to us, there had only ever been one high-rise condominium (the Meridian), and the sales velocity of that project was modest, to say the least.

The environment for luxury high-rise condominium development was murky at best. But I was being hailed by some of the local boosters as a "visionary," bringing big-city living to a city that was ready to embrace its future—as soon as it could get the homeless, the drunks, and the bums off the would-be construction site.

Rule #291: Beware the word "visionary." It often means someone who desperately needs new glasses.

The good news about the Meridian is that at least it was a "comparable," and it allowed me to show prospective venture partners that I was not the first idiot to want to do this. In fact, I was following in the footsteps of the dumb guy before us who had previously misjudged the market and walked off the cliff, but I was going to use a longer rope so things were going to work out just great. Trust me.

And so we get to the hot, muggy, crappy summer of 1988 in Los Angeles, where Rule #3 kicks in. This is the most important rule in the book. Pay close attention.

Rule #3: You must go to every meeting and every event, in particular the ones you know for sure will be a total waste of time.

This rule sounds a bit "zenny" but the truth is it is the one rule from which all greatness and success spring forth.

Psychoanalysts have opined in this area in many ways, but what clearly happens is when you expect nothing and know for sure that nothing good can happen, that this next period in your life is in fact, absolutely for certain, bound to be a total and complete waste of time and further, that you have no interest in going, attending, or participating in the event, it is then, and only then, that you are totally and completely open and available for greatness to appear and be thrust upon you. All you have to do is stand there and hang on and it will, more often than not, show up, and if you do not close your eyes or swat it away in stupidity—if you embrace it, engage it, wonder at it, accept it, and finally connect to it—the universe will appear before you and you will be ready to proceed into the realm of good things happening.

The corollary to Rule #3 is **Rule #217: You don't know what you don't know.**

This rule will appear frequently.

The negotiating agreement had a provision that required us to put up $500,000 on or before September 20, 1988. If we failed to do that (after having gotten three extensions), the Redevelopment Agency was going to pull the plug on the deal and pick someone else to do the project. In simple English, we would be out on our asses, and all the money we had invested would be converted into banjo picks.

So I am sitting in my small office on Sawtelle Avenue in Los Angeles, puzzling over my stellar impersonation of Stan Hardy: "Here's another fine mess you've gotten me into." (I had left the savings and loan a year earlier. I could see the handwriting on the wall—there was no possible way they could have this much leverage and not blow up into smithereens.)

Funny how history repeats itself.

Given my former position at Brookside, I was still on some sucker mailing lists, and sure enough, I get an invitation to go to a lunch in honor of Thomas Spiegel, who was then CEO of Columbia Savings and Loan. They were honoring him for something, and there would be a few speeches but mostly there would be 400 people under a tent on a miserably hot day, trying to suck at the tit of "done deal," with traffic and parking aggravation and I knew it was stupid and a total waste of time, but after all, it was a free meal and I had nothing going so . . . WTF, I'm there for you, baby.

Rule #2: Networking is a profession. Become a professional at it.

This rule, along with Rule #3, form the core foundation for success. If you are going to adhere to Rule #3 and actually go to something stupid and dehumanizing and miserable, then goddamnit, you better strap on Rule #2 big time and work the room like a mother-fucker. Networking is a serious business. It requires fortitude and practice. There are 123 books written on the subject. Get a couple, read them, and practice. Networking is like hitting golf balls on the range: after you have hit four buckets, get serious and hit four more.

The lunch was held in a large white tent in the parking lot of the savings and loan (like I said, parking was a bitch) and there was a lavish buffet and lots of booze. (Two drinks on a hot Tuesday afternoon and you are ready to pass out and take a nap.)

The drink lines were long, the speeches were long. Yes, it's true Tom is a leader and a visionary blah blah and he and his pal Mike Milken were changing the world of finance as we knew it. Yadda yadda . . .

Finally, you get to stand in one more line: the buffet food line.

Rule #248: When standing in a buffet line, everybody lies a little. By the time you get to the pasta salad, everybody lies a lot.

So I am in line waiting and the guy in back of me says, "What are you working on?"

This is what people say when real estate guys get together. Everyone has a great deal to discuss because everyone is working on something that needs money but that will make even more money if they get the money to do the deal.

Money and deals go together like soap and water (but in prison, beware of the soap thing).

So I tell the guy that I have a big piece of land tied up in down-town San Diego, high-rise luxury, residential, near the water, across from convention center, "A" location, city loves me, got my approvals, I am there for you, baby. And oh, by the way, I only need to deliver a simple letter of credit for $500,000 on September 20 (78 days away). Otherwise the city fathers and CCDC will call my bluff, and I will know for sure that Harry only fired five shots and I will lose all my entitlements and I will certainly lose the $750,000 that my partners and I have already pissed away on lawyers and architects and consultants and engineering and whatever.

"You just keep thinking, Butch. That's what you're good at."
—*Butch Cassidy and the Sundance Kid*

And all of a sudden, the din of the room silences, and this fellow behind me in line says the magic words that have fueled the fantasies of dreamers from time immemorial: "Sounds great. I know the perfect partner for you."

Take a breath. This is a true story.

The one dumb sonofabitch out of 400 people happens to be standing right behind me in line rubbing the magic genie lamp while waiting to get to the pasta salad.

So I say, "Swell, that sounds just great. Would you like to go ahead of me? The pasta salad looks terrific."

We exchange business cards, the lunch ends, and I go back to the office and call this guy, expecting to hear someone from the psychiatric ward at the UCLA Medical Center answer the phone. But nope, in fact, this guy actually was a real person (after all, someone answered his phone) and when you are looking for a Mae West, you don't argue about the color of the life jacket.

And so it began on July 13, 1988. Seventy-eight days to go.

The young man proceeds to introduce me to his client, Bruce Stark. Mr. Stark was in fact at that time a very big, successful, high-rise residential developer in Hawaii. Over the previous 12 years, he had built seven high-rises—contemporary, tall, thin, sexy buildings—and had sold out every one of them at high prices per square foot and, no question, he was rich and famous.

And the craziest thing of all: he was in the mood, wanted to come to the mainland, ready to do a big deal, bring it. So, he and his entourage fly over from Honolulu to San Diego to do some due diligence. It is August. Plenty of time. I line up all the players involved in this deal, from CCDC to members of the city council. Mr. Stark is in the house and let freedom ring.

I am waving my arms in double time, painting the vision of the city by the bay and what it would look like after Mr. Stark puts his imprint on it. Greatness was available for the taking.

At the end of the two days, we sit down for that most famous of all times: the right-before-you-are-getting-on-the-plane-and-would-you-mind-telling-me-just-where-the-fuck-do-I-actually-stand time. I mean, I can hear the train coming down the track, and Pauline is tied up pretty tight.

"I like it. I am inclined to do this deal with you, but one thing you need to understand—your design stinks. We will need to redesign the entire building. If I am going to put my name on this project, it has to be world-class and it has to have the signature Stark design."

(Listen, pal, you can paint the fucking thing pink if you want. Just give me the $500,000.)

"I totally agree with you, Mr. Stark. It would be an honor to work with you and be a small part of the greatness that you could bring to America's Finest City." Yadda yadda.

Rule #144: You made your bed, now you have to lie in it—even if the sheets are dirty.

By now, the savings and loan business had become the savings and loan mess, and in fact the government was having discussions with both of my partners in this deal, concerning some minor, technical, obscure rules that they seemed to have bent a bit while they were running the savings and loan. I guess they weren't too obscure because Michael ended up doing a short stint in the big house later on—but at that time we had a more pressing problem.

Rule #404: What seems like a problem is often nothing more than an opportunity looking to be found.

Stark was making all the right noises, but how could the City of San Diego do business with people of questionable character, namely my two partners from the savings and loan?

(Listen, City, you were doing business with me, so let's not get too righteous here.)

Still, this deal involved City money and we needed to brush our hound's teeth extra clean. "So, angel, you're taking the fall," with Mr. Pastel and Mr. Moers playing the part of Brigid O'Shaughnessy.

The feds weren't chasing my ass, so I was sort of OK, but my partners had to take a powder. But after all, they still had $500,000 in this deal—and fair is fair. Unfortunately, they also had a few legal bills from battling the boys with the eye shades, so they were in the mood to take a modest haircut and get out of Dodge.

Still, it was not clear where I was going to get the shears.

My partners were not true believers that this deal would ever really happen, so when I offered to pay them off with $300,000, they agreed. Then I suggested that since I didn't have any money, would they take a note for that amount, secured by my interest in the property (which, if Stark did not fund, would be worth zero).

My partners agreed, and I was now free to see if could boat the great white Stark alone.

Rule #260: When someone very smart does something for you that seems dumb, remember to say thank you; they are not stupid.

My partners were some of the shrewdest real estate guys I have ever met. Michael, in particular, is off-the-chart smart. To this day, I know that they made that deal with me not because they were dumb, but because they wanted to give me a break, a chance to have my own score. They both had made some serious money, I had not yet—and so in telling the story, do not think how dumb they were to take a worthless note, rather think about how gracious they were. And to this day, and for always, I am grateful. There is only one response: Thank you.

Rule #95: Don't forget. Short-term memory loss or revisionist history does not cut it.

Seven years later, I turned back to Michael and made him a partner in another deal of mine. His ROI on that deal was 800 percent. I remembered; we're all square.

So now I had the usual 12 balls in the air: straddling my partners who wanted out, begging Mr. Stark who I wanted in, stalling the redevelopment agency who wanted some money, stalling the lawyers and architects who wanted their bills paid. Everyone could sense that the kid was running out of tricks.

And then Mr. Stark invited me to Hawaii. We were going to discuss making the deal. I was being invited into the inner sanctum to see the buildings he had built—and to discuss money.

I took a 6 a.m. flight from San Diego to Honolulu. It was a wonderful, sunny, pleasant day, and I will tell you that Bruce Stark was and is a gentleman and could not have been more gracious and charming.

Rule #122: It is always more fun to date than it is to get married.

By 5 p.m., we had made a deal and off we went to a fancy dinner with his entire entourage, the team that was going to be responsible for this great adventure in San Diego. His team was very talented.

After dessert, he asked me if he could take me back to my hotel, and I told him I had booked the red-eye back to San Diego. I had been in Hawaii for 12 hours, made what would turn out to be a $90 million deal, and flew home. I have been back to Hawaii just once in the ensuing 25 years, and that was only because my wife won a free trip.

The deal was coming together, and it was now the first week of September.

A lot of lawyers and phone calls and faxes (no e-mail, remember, this was 1988) and finally on Thursday, September 19, the day before the hearing on the 20th when I needed to show up with the dough, Bruce Stark wired $800,000—enough to pay off my partners and fund the letter of credit, and on that Friday morning, I flew down to San Diego from L.A. on the 6 a.m. flight and walked into the CCDC hearing at 8:25 a.m. They went through some formalities, then announced our item and a motion was made to put up or shut up. I walked up to Ms. Pam Hamilton, the executive director, handed her a check for $500,000 made out to CCDC and then just like in the movies, I turned to the august group on the dais and said, "We are ready to proceed." Hell, we had 20 minutes to spare!

I'm there for you, baby.

Rule #297: Fuck the fat lady singing. It is never over.

Thus began two more years of haggling, deals, loans, redesign, renegotiation, and more lawyers and architects and egos.

Mr. Stark came to this adventure with a couple of his own henchmen-type characters, his own version of Haldeman and Ehrlichman. Say hello to Mr. Stacy Wong and Mr. David McCurdy.

And I receded into a more minor role. I was the point person in San Diego but the big decisions were driven by the Stark team. Still, I had a 25 percent interest in the dog, I was supposed to get some fees, and I did not have to fund any more money, and I didn't have to guarantee the loan; in retrospect an amazing deal (and I knew it). After all, I was a guy who knew how to build a two-story, wood-frame, garden apartment house, and now I was co-developer of a 40-story high-rise luxury condominium tower.

Rule #109: Never let the truth get in the way of a good story.

For the next two years, the project progressed until finally in early 1990, Home Federal Savings and Loan (they aren't around anymore either—another savings and loan that found itself in a bit of a bind) lent us $89.5 million to build One Harbor Drive.

I signed on the loan. No guarantee, just my signature along with a good faith promise to actually complete the project. I liked signing on the loan; it made me feel like a real developer, a full partner. Home Fed had lots of marble floors, lots of lawyers, lots of paperwork, and lots of money (at least at that time). The closing dinner was fantastic, fueled by fantasies and visions of sugar plums laced with multi-million dollar floor-to-ceiling glass culminating in an orgiastic explosion in which every cell in the spreadsheet was multiplied by four, and the profits were so large (on paper) that my share was an easy ticket to NetJets.

Signing on the loan will prove to be very important.

Rule #139: If you borrow $5,000 and don't pay it back, the bank will come after you; they are the lender and you are the borrower, and you promised you would pay them back the money. They will track you to the darkest cave in Afghanistan. If you borrow $100 million and can't pay it back, the bank might come after you—but at that point, they are not really your lender any more, *they are your partner.*

By the middle of 1991, the project is underway and coming out of the ground and it is pretty impressive. There is a really big, deep hole, lots of steel and concrete, cranes and trailers, and a development team with dreams of very large sale prices per square foot.

But the henchmen and I were not doing so well. Stark stayed in Hawaii most of the time, while the Bobbsey Twins stayed in town and relayed phone calls and faxes to headquarters detailing every twist and turn, each vying for the love of their boss. And whenever there was a problem, somehow it was my fault.

Rule #84: Sucking up to the king works best when you can throw someone else under the bus to enhance your own position.

In the real estate business, there is one rule above all others that needs to be tattooed on a developer's forehead (or on his stomach by Ms. Salander) and that is:

Rule #313: *DO NOT BELIEVE YOUR OWN BULLSHIT.*

You have to understand that real estate development is a game wherein you make a bunch of rosy projections and then you sell those projections to your equity partner and to your bank, hoping to get 100 percent financing, so you have none of your own money in the deal, so you can leverage the shit out of the project, and put the majority of the risk on the dumb sonofabitch lender—and the lender in turn tries to figure out where the lies are being told, where the assumptions are false, and then they decide how much to believe of the projections, and then based on how much they believe and how badly they need the fees, they give you money to actually build the project, hoping that when the thing is done, you can actually sell or rent whatever it is for rates that are close to or better than the ones you put in the pro-forma, which is now in a drawer somewhere, waiting for litigation or celebration.

I was such a fierce believer in Rule #313 that I literally put it on my wall. It is critical in all games of chance to properly assess reality and truth—not the distorted dreams and hopes of the last-gasp gambler. Do not believe your own bullshit.

I am very good at numbers.

And I knew that some of our projections were rosy; not false, you understand, but optimistic. When we made them the market was stronger, but now that we were coming out of the ground, and the real estate recession was gathering steam, that rosy stuff began to look a bit peaked. In my humble opinion, we were entering a phase known as the dichotomous alternate reality, which is a psychiatric term that loosely translated means "Take the money and run."

Rule #453: Do not trust the appraiser or the rating agencies. An appraisal is an opinion of value, provided by someone who has no money in the deal, who gets paid long before the final scorecard is tallied. If he is wrong, he is usually not around to pick up any small shards of glass and you will probably be left holding various large pieces of luggage. Think Moody's, Standard and Poor's, along with the guy who said we could sell these condominiums for $600 per square foot.

I had become a bit of a pest to the Stark team. I kept making suggestions based on my view of reality (e.g., floor-to-ceiling height) and they kept telling me to shut up, go away little boy, don't bother us, we know exactly what we are doing, after all, we have built 10 million square feet of high-rise residential, and you have built zero, so go back in your hole and put a lid on it.

I have issues with lids.

So we get to late 1991, and the two henchmen are swiftly moving me to persona non grata status with the big boss. They are poisoning Stark's ear (shades of Hamlet) with tales of my becoming a political liability.

And then *deus ex machina* shows up in the form of a California Department of Real Estate White Paper error with respect to the very complicated condominium parcel map that we had filed. I can no longer remember the legal issue, but the key element was simple. We needed to amend the loan documents and to do that required the signature of all the partners, of which, as you remember, I was one. Bruce was going to need the kid's signature, the same kid who had been walking around town with a lid on his head.

Rule #192: "What we've got here is a failure to communicate." —*Cool Hand Luke*

Now, you remember about that dichotomous alternate reality. "Bruce, I've been thinking, I know that our relations have been a bit strained of late, and the truth is your boys (henchmen) are doing a fine job here in town, and if this project is going to be the huge success that you feel it will be, maybe it would be in your best (perceived) self-interest to buy me out. Then you wouldn't have to be bothered (putting up with my nagging the shit out of you about how the thing you are building is not going to sell the way you think it is) with any minority partners with respect to your vision and key decisions."

"Well," Abe said, "where d'ya want this killin' done?"

God said, "Out on Highway 61."

And Bruce said he would take it under advisement.

By now, I was feeling that this dog had failure written all over it. The real estate market that had been robust in 1989 was losing steam in 1991. And I could see that when the dust settled I was going to be dust.

So while Bruce was cogitating, the two henchmen asked me to sign the revised loan docs. They needed to file the amended documents with the state. The timing was important because A depended on B and B depended on C and C had to happen before M could . . . yadda yadda.

Rule #78: "If you have them by the balls, their hearts and minds will follow." This rule is credited to General William Westmoreland and his assessment of the likelihood of our success in Vietnam.

And so in the fall of 1991, Mr. Stark flew over to have dinner with me and discuss my suggestion.

We sat in the corner booth of Rainwater's, a famous downtown watering hole. *Mano a mano*—no henchmen. I had rehearsed and prepared for this part my entire life. The bald soprano and the fireman were back on stage once again.

We ordered steaks—big, red meat, testosterone-fueled, check-your-penis-at-the-door steaks. (I do not particularly care for steak, but there was no wussing out with chicken when you were going for the *estocada*.)

He talked. I listened. He could not have been more charming. He was enjoying himself.

Rule #403: Use your opponent's power to keep returning the ball back to him.

Early in the evening, Bruce answered a question and it was at that point that I knew I had the game won.

"What is it like being a big-time developer?" I asked.

Rule #29: It never hurts to pitch one down the middle early with a little ego balm on it.

"I have been doing real estate deals my whole life. It is who I am and what I know . . . and the sad part is, it is an unforgiving and ruthless business. You're only as good as your last deal. Like a shark has to swim, if I didn't do deals, I would die."

His reasoning and decision to buy me out was informed by history, by ego, by self-aggrandizement, by self-image. And my decision to sell had only one simple component: I didn't want to end up with nothing.

Rule #119: "I made all my money by selling too soon." —J. Pierpont Morgan

Rule #244: Clarity of thinking is improved when there is only one variable in play.

The entire negotiation took nine days. Bruce Stark is not a man to trifle with. He made an offer, I countered, he made another offer. And although he never said anything about take it or leave it, I knew that there would not be a third offer.

Rule #305: Know your opponent's style, and adapt your game to his. You need lots of different shots; you can't just play big serve and volley.

Some guys would want to negotiate this for a couple months, arguing about nuances—like what would happen if it rained on a Thursday in Des Moines, and who would pay for the umbrella, or should we just buy LL Bean waterproof shoes. What I knew about

Mr. Stark was you were only going to get two bites at the apple; he was not a man to make applesauce.

Rule #99: Waiting is more painful than a proctology exam. The first person to talk loses.

Four days passed after offer #2. Had I blown it? Finally, he called back. He split the difference with a slight nod to my number.

Rule #120: You can't go broke taking a profit.

He offered to pay me a few million dollars, with a down payment and a series of payments over 12 months. I'm there for you, baby. Done and done.

If I had horsed him around for one more round, I would have gotten nothing; he was a two-bite guy—no more, period.

On paper I had sold my 25 percent interest for 17 percent of the projected profit. The key word here is "projected." "Projected" is what was showing on the internal assumptions of the spreadsheet, the appraisal, the pro-forma to the bank. My number was the future reality of the project filtered through the lens of a discounted net present value, sweetened by the deep desire to have no partners. If it were going to be a grand slam, why share if you don't have to.

Twenty-four months later the building fell into foreclosure, there was litigation and pain, and Stark and his henchmen ended up with nothing.

A couple years later, I learned an interesting fact about Mr. Stark. In all his deals, he had always bought out his original partners. He never finished with the same guys he started with.

I had a grubstake now and, as they say at the craps table, it was time to "press the eight."

Nota bene: In October 2010, I take my beautiful wife, Ms. Bry, to Las Vegas to celebrate our 10th wedding anniversary. We stay at the Four Seasons and when we arrive around 1:30 p.m., we decide to have lunch, alfresco, on the patio. I am facing her. We have been seated for a while. All of a sudden, I hear a voice, a voice that I have heard before, a voice that I will never forget. I turn around and there, six feet away at the next table, sits Bruce Stark, surrounded by three gorgeous women, all of them having lunch.

I get up and re-introduce myself to him. He stands up and hugs me affectionately, introduces me to the ladies, and proudly proclaims that I was the one who helped him do the project in San Diego. He spoke with pride about the high-rise and he was clearly proud of our effort there. And then he embraced me one last time.

It was striking to me: After 20 years, his recollection was an especially fond one. After all, he was, is, and always will be a real estate developer. It is his DNA. It is who he is.

Bruce Stark is one of the most remarkable men I have ever met. And without question, one of the most charming.

CHAPTER 4

ARROGANCE

(DAMN, STUPID ARROGANCE!)

Rule #100: If you are running down a road and you look back and there is no one following you, there are two—and only two—possibilities. One, you are way the hell ahead. Two, you are on the wrong road.

And that brings us to the infamous Pacific Coast Highway deal. After getting a few dollars from Mr. Stark, I naturally assumed that I was a genius and could make no mistakes and that everything I would or could touch in downtown San Diego would turn to gold.

Real estate was nothing more than a game of leverage and zoning approvals and financing terms and knowing the market. Nothing more except the 39 other things that come into play and that you can only vaguely control. I was a downtown "player" now, and I was the guy you brought a deal to when it "had some hair on it."

"Had some hair" is a euphemism for a deal that is fucked up—unbuildable, unreasonable seller, litigation, adverse zoning, toxic—you name it. If the deal was hairy, the brokers brought it to me. And I loved it. Because I really didn't have much money, so I needed to outthink the competition. If you are a REIT (real estate investment trust) or a big company like Tishman Speyer with $500 million in the bank, you can actually pay for things. You can just write a check and actually close. If you are a small time hustler/pisher, the only way you can create incremental value is by applying brains instead of brawn.

Rule #82: A can opener beats using your teeth every time.

It was 1991, the market was cooling, but I was still trying to tie up every piece of land downtown with long escrows and time to maneuver before I had to actually write a significant check.

My modus operandi was simple. I had to identify a deal that was currently lousy but that with some maneuvering and some luck could become valuable, and then convince the seller that I could actually close, but that I needed a bit more time than the infamous "15 days' due diligence, close in 30 for all cash" model that had existed during the go-go years of the mid-1980s.

Even though it would take a bit more time to close, if a seller rode my horse, he would get a better deal. Then simultaneously (as the ink was drying on the escrow papers) I began to race around the country trying to find someone who had real money who would become my partner, explaining to that partner that if he rode my horse, he would have an easier time getting approvals and I would provide domain expertise, feet on the street, the secret handshake, the political grease, the map of where the bodies were buried.

Rule #219: All that riding will wear out a few pair of horseshoes. Find a good blacksmith.

To get paid for "having figured it out and gotten the approvals" required working the deal, making the seller crazy, extending and renegotiating the terms several times, scrambling, begging, threatening litigation, until finally you assemble all the necessary moving pieces and are ready to actually hand over the dough. And then, like a magician, you pull the cover off the birdcage to reveal not the one white dove you expected, but five new white doves. At that same precise moment you close and record the loan, close the equity, pull the building permit, and turn the first shovel of dirt at the site. Zero carry. That is the art of the real estate development deal.

My blacksmith at that time was Brian Seltzer, an absolutely relentless real estate attorney. It was the perfect marriage. I believed in leverage and the double straddle. He believed in legal fees and airtight contracts. There was a third crony in our gang, Jack Guttman, a tough contractor, who believed in nothing. Together we formed the Relentless Pursuit Club. We were the only three members. We could never find another person who qualified for membership.

Rule #218: Grand passion (and relentless pursuit) will take you further than good grades.

As a gag, we made up some T-shirts, with the word "relentless" on the front and "pursuit" on the back. Eight years later I was giving a speech to the San Diego Venture Group on the subject of venture capitalists and how to land one. I walked up to the podium, took off my dress shirt and put on the T-shirt, modeling it front and back. They got the message. And then I threw a half dozen into the audience the same way the Pad Squad throws T-shirts into the stands at a Padres home baseball game. When all is said and done, real estate is a simple game. Hit the ball, throw the ball, catch the ball.

In retrospect, I may have missed my calling. I should have been a lawyer, defending the poor and innocent in the courtroom, ripping justice from the hearts of the evil and greedy. Instead I became an expert at reading and writing real estate contracts. And in every contract, there were always a few fishhooks. It was just part of the game. You had to keep the other side honest.

Rule #292: There is a fishhook in every deal. If you cannot find the fishhook, then do not take the bait.

Allow me to introduce you to Mr. Dominic Calabrese, a charming man who owned another oddball piece of dirt (shaped in an L with a small cut-out for a gay bathhouse in the back corner) across from the County Administration Building on Pacific Highway in downtown San Diego. The game plan was right out of Chapter 3 of the Relentless Pursuit playbook: get a toehold on the land, then acquire the rest of the dirt, get rid of the bathhouse, get approvals, etc., and voila, build a lovely mid-priced hotel . . . yadda yadda.

Rule #432: If you think "yadda yadda" is a substitute for rigorous thinking, you are about to lose your shirt.

The terms and conditions were classic: small down payment, lots of time. But this time I got sloppy and arrogant, and made a critical error. Instead of accruing the interest payments, I agreed to make current semi-annual payments on the note, which meant I would have to come out of personal pocket with some dough every six months until I could find a partner. I had rules, but I broke one of them. Very expensive lesson.

Rule #18: Rules are not made to be broken.

I love partners. My model has always been partners. I have done all my deals with partners. Before I became a real estate developer, I spent nine years in Hollywood, writing screenplays and sit-coms (very few ever got made) but I had a writing partner. I did dialogue; he did plot.

Bottom line: I like partners.

So I tied up the Calabrese land and went looking for a partner. And I could not find one. Not a single one of the usual suspects thought this was a good deal. There was not a true believer in the whole lot of them. I drew pictures and explained and modeled and spreadsheeted but no one would come in on the 150K down payment and the carry.

Twenty years later, much has been written about crowd sourcing and the wisdom of crowds. You remember the rule? If you are running down a road and there is no one behind you . . .

I was not way the fuck ahead; I was on the wrong road.

It was about this time that my wife began to have doubts about the particular lifestyle I had picked. We had just made some real money for the first time from Mr. Stark, and before the body was cold I was rolling more dough into another deal. It made her nuts.

It is no different than finding out you are married to an addict. I did not take pills or gamble or do drugs or buy fancy watches or fast cars—but I had a very fast pen. I liked deals.

Rule #308: Deal making can be a fatal disease. But, it's the cure that might kill you.

Remember it was Bruce Stark who said he was only as good as his last deal, and that was the key to winning the negotiation. And then I went off and committed the exact same neurotic sin by chasing the next deal before I had even cashed his second check. Crazy.

Another fatal error had also emerged on this deal. I had assumed that Mr. Calabrese, a nice older Italian gentleman, soft spoken, charming, a bit naïve, would be easy to manipulate, that I could extend and bend and that he would be a roll-over.

Rule #112: There is a reason that the Mafia are Italian.

The only rolling over that occurred in this deal was when his truck rolled over my leg and broke my kneecap.

Meet Mussolini. I must have been out of my mind. The guy was a delight to spend time with. I had at least a dozen meals with him, smiling and drinking, but when the market turned rotten and I needed more time and less payments and gimme a break, what he said was, "A deal's a deal."

What! Where did he learn that? That concept was downright un-American. Where was Joe McCarthy when you needed him? Imagine those words ringing in my ears. Huh, you want to *stick to the deal we signed*? What about the disappearing ink pen? A man's word is his bond? What if the bond was secured by Lehman Brothers or Donald Trump? Can you spell default, followed by cram down, and then the exchange of debt for equity?

What was he talking about? A deal is not a deal. A deal is only the beginning of a deal that needs to be dealt with for a longer time and no deal is ever done and what do you mean, you are foreclosing on me?

The loss was $492,000. After 36 months of maneuvering and spinning, as the real estate market got worser and worser, I ran out of tricks. Toast. Leave the keys on the bathhouse door and don't honk.

Rule #249: If you can't find a partner willing to get in the boat and go over the falls with you, then maybe the boat leaks. You didn't bring a patch kit?

Now this rule has some exceptions. Sometimes you have to follow your own star. Group think should mostly be avoided; Van Gogh was not recognized as a genius until after he died. But for most of us regular, average everyday deal guys, the following rule is pretty solid.

Rule #281: If no one else will jump in the pool, then look down first and see if there is any water in it before you launch off the high board doing a backflip with a 2½ twist.

Pacific Highway taught me my arrogance, my greed, my stupidity, my failure, my shame.

Rule #336: When you do something really dumb, make sure you remember it so you don't ever do it again.

I really wanted to remember this one. I did not go for the Salander tattoo model but I got close. Every year I had to do a net worth statement for the bank, and for the next 10 years I carried this deal, Pacific Highway, LLC, on my net worth statement at zero because I wanted to be reminded every year just how incredibly dumb that deal had been. Every year for 10 years I had the glorious opportunity to look at that line on the statement with its goose egg—and to remember.

Rule #412: Do not sweep the dogs under the rug. Hang them on your wall right next to the moose head.

I have gone to a hundred events where people tell me how smart they are and how they did this, did that, and then voila, they ended with $200 million. Bullshit squared. What I want to know is the failures. Don't tell me how smart you are. That is boring and mostly dishonest. Rather, tell me how dumb you are. Those are the lessons that move men's souls because it leads you to your own humanity and brings you into the community. In the deal business, if you bat .650 you are an MVP. No one bats .1000.

Rule #197: The lessons of life are expensive and painful. They cannot be bought on the cheap. Do not demean them. Treasure them and cherish them and announce them—you will feel better afterward and you will be able to look your kids in the eye.

Rule #200: After a decade you can take the hair shirt off your net worth statement. After all, even purgatory does not last for eternity.

CHAPTER 5

FAILURE IS AN OPTION

Let me remind you of a man named Gene Krantz, who was the head of Mission Control in 1970 when Apollo 13 ran into a small problem. An oxygen tank in the lunar module blew up and astronaut Jim Lovell called Krantz and calmly said, "Houston, we have a problem."

It appeared the boys could not get back to Earth. And it was Krantz who famously rallied the troops in the NASA control center and told them, "Failure is not an option."

But is this really true? Isn't failure always an option and, in fact, shouldn't it be? Without the possibility of failure, there is by definition a diminished chance for success.

Take something simple like learning to ride a bicycle. When you go from a tricycle to a two-wheeler, you fall a lot before you figure it out. You fail and then you succeed. And then riding a bike becomes like sex. No matter how long it is between rides, you don't forget how to do it.

According to Krantz who wrote the book *Failure Is Not an Option*, failure should always be on the table. It was always at the top of the discussions at NASA. He asked his engineers to perform miracles, but as he said, "Hoping is no substitute for process and planning," and so NASA always had a backup plan.

One thing that Krantz talks about in the book is that things that went well and looked effortless often had behind them hair-raising, last-minute, seat-of-the-pants decisions that frequently were greatly influenced by sheer dumb luck.

I warn you: Never underestimate the power of luck.

In the case of a public and prestigious action like a moon shot, that phrase, "Failure is not an option," may have served as an important morale booster, but for most of us failure always lurks somewhere in the cards, like the Black Queen in the card game Hearts, or in the case of Wall Street, The Black Swan theory articulated by Nassim Nicholas Taleb.

Had the boys from Bear, Lehman, Merrill, and AIG only read Taleb's book on risk. Given what we now know, I think one could safely say that failure was not an option; it was inevitable.

Success is measured by failure. And failure in and of itself can be a transformational event, an experience that makes us reflect on life and all that jazz about what's important and family and friends and whether or not we should do this insane thing called a start-up one more time.

I always think of Nietzsche, who said, "That which does not kill us makes us stronger."

But remember Nietzsche never had to interact with venture capitalists. If he had, he would have written *Dante's Inferno*.

In the fall of 2006, I was flying to New Hampshire where 12 members of my company were hard at work. The company, Quanlight, was trying to make a unique kind of red light-emitting diode (LED) chip, and in my briefcase I had seven termination letters with final paychecks. We had been searching for venture capital for nine months with no success. We had contacted 21 VC firms, we had pitched to 15 of them and had been told to drop dead by 14 of those, with one firm, located in Canada, expressing mild interest from a newbie partner who had been with the firm only eight months and had never done a deal with the firm—not the most promising of likelihoods.

In the meantime, my glorious wife, Ms. Barbara Bry, had begun to notice that I was miserable every night when I came home, that I had begun to take sleeping pills, that I was kicking the cat, and that I was not much fun to be around.

We had raised $4 million from angels and $2 million from a corporate venture capitalist, and I personally knew most all of the angels and I was not looking forward to telling them that we were going to liquidate, close the doors, bail out, and give them back 10 cents on the dollar if we could even find someone who would buy the intellectual property, which was incomplete and still didn't work the way it was supposed to.

I had failures in my past—we all do—and I wasn't looking forward to another one.

And I was not going to fool myself; not at my age. That old bromide that you learn from failures, that failures make you stronger, that you are human and humans make mistakes didn't work for me, and neither did the rationale that after all, Quanlight was difficult technology and it hadn't been done before and we were trying to challenge the laws of physics and after all tomorrow is another day. Bullshit. Maybe there was another day for Scarlett but not for me.

This start-up/innovation/next big thing/change the world game—is it really worth it?

I think what drives entrepreneurs is neither fame nor fortune; it is revenge. You want to show your music teacher who gave you a C-minus or your mother who thought you were an idiot or your first wife who left you when you were broke. You want to show them. It is seeking the adrenalin rush, the mainline search for validation and success. It is the need to put the needle in one more time and get high from the death-defying spiral as you seek once again to pull it out of the fire, nail the homer into the upper deck, sink the shot at the buzzer, the "He shoots, he scores!" syndrome—the John Elway/Joe Montana effect—90 yards to go, less than two minutes to play. Gimme the ball.

It is what entrepreneurs do. The statistics are terrible, and the odds are long. No one wants to be told that you have less than a 10 percent chance of making any money from a start-up. In 2010, the top quartile of venture capitalists have an average return of minus 2 percent, i.e., to be in the top 25 percent of your class, all you have to do is give back 98 cents on the dollar—after seven years. Gimme a break.

I like the idea that people are in charge of their destiny and fate. It is an appealing idea and belief, but I am here to tell you that much of life is random. And to a large extent, we are influenced not by quantum physics, but by the random movement of the molecules of luck.

I got to the lab in New Hampshire but I couldn't pull the trigger. Too much hope in the air. I flew home with the termination letters in my briefcase.

But after 45 days of denial, anger, bargaining, guilt, and depression, I finally decided that I would in fact throw in the towel, close the company, return the money we still had in the bank, and lick my wounds in a small, padded cell on some deserted island. We were done.

A few days after later, I was standing in the parking lot outside my shrink's office on my way to discuss the best way to kill myself, when I checked my Blackberry to find an e-mail from a corporate venture capitalist, Micron Ventures (the venture arm of Micron Technologies).

Remember **Rule #1:** Return every e-mail and every phone call.

So I called the guy right then and there and he said he was interested in "learning more about the company." That was the standard VC waste of time, poking around kind of inquiry.

So I told him, "Look, pal, I'm not going to waste my time with you if all you want to do is make me crazy, pick my brain, and then humiliate and reject me. I'm not in the mood. Go away."

There was a pause and he said, "Well, what do you need?"

So I told him. I needed $5 million, a foundry, some more technical geniuses, production and distribution facilities. And if I could get it in the next couple weeks, that would be great.

Whereupon he said, "I think maybe we can do that for you."

I told him I was late for the shrink and that I would call him back later.

Six weeks after that morning, we had negotiated an investment, a license, and an acquisition deal with an $8 billion semiconductor company.

Like I told you earlier, don't ever discount luck.

As we got ready to fly up and sign all the documents, I thought back on the 21 venture capitalists who told me to die and pound sand. And all that crap they handed out about only doing deals with 10 times returns and needing to build big companies and IPOs and billion dollar markets—it's just that—crap! The VC geniuses remind me of what William Goldman, a famous screenwriter said about Hollywood, "Nobody knows nothing."

Nota bene: In fact, after another three weeks of negotiation, the deal blew up in our faces. And I made the final decision to close the company and return the remaining money to the investors. It was clear we were never going to get there from here, at least not this time.

Rule #44: Don't spend investor money if there is no hope. Give it back. They will remember the kindness in the future.

Nota bene: We recently filed a lawsuit against Micron Technologies. I'll let you know how that works out in Volume Two.

CHAPTER 6

NEVER DISCOUNT THE POSSIBILITY OF INSANITY FROM THE OTHER SIDE

Rule #195: You can defer legal fees but you cannot avoid them.

I agree with most American business leaders that the last thing America needs more of is lawyers. And of course, Shakespeare is famous for his line from *Henry VI*: "The first thing we do, let's kill all the lawyers."

At last count, there were 2,347,112 lawyer jokes on Google. That is a lot of laughter at a billable rate somewhere between 125 and 1,000 bucks per hour. At those rates, there is nothing to laugh about.

However, if you ask my peer group what they think of lawyers, you will hear unmitigated fury and disdain, followed by this mantra: "Except my lawyer, Joe Smith, who is absolutely fabulous." We hate the other guy with a fury, but our personal hair stylist? Fantastic!

In my case, the lawyer in question is Brian Seltzer. I met Brian in 1985 when I first came to San Diego and tied up the odd-shaped L block that later became the Harbor Drive high-rise residential towers, a.k.a. Bruce Stark's waterloo.

He was young (I guess I was too) and wickedly smart, and as I have said before, it was a match made in legal heaven: that place where the finest minds are righteously sent out each morning, armed with a word processor, to do battle for their clients in the unrequited hope that like Clarence Oddbody (*It's a Wonderful Life*), they too will ring the bell and earn their wings.

I stayed with him for 16 years until finally my real estate adventures had wound down to nothing more than a condo in Pacific Beach in which three lovely ladies have been living for the last seven years. I have never met them. They pay the rent, and I don't ask any questions.

Brian was one of the smartest real estate lawyers in town at that time, and he was hungry and creative. "Creative" is a code word for someone who actually reads the document and then reads between the lines of the document and then tries to find that small crack of light between those lines—sort of like Bill Clinton's nuanced answer, "It depends on what the meaning of the word 'is' is."

Brian and I never, ever crossed the line into illegal but together we were able to press right up to the line, peek over the edge, and take advantage of not just the law but the irrational behavior of the other side.

Rule #302: More money is lost through neurotic behavior than through bad business decisions.

Now, my favorite author of all time is not Hemingway nor Faulkner nor Roth nor Bellow. I was an English major and I have read them all cover to cover. The most profitable author I have ever read is Daniel Kahneman. Danny Boy won the Nobel Prize in economics in 2002 for a piece of work describing how people make decisions.

We all know that the basis for rational economic behavior is the assumption that each of us will attempt to act in our own best-perceived self-interest. The key word here is *"perceived."* It is the study of this word that provides the greatest opportunity for wealth and success. I believe deeply, strongly, and irrevocably that the majority of us do not properly perceive what is in our best self-interest.

Consider the opportunities that abound for stupid and misguided decision making: marriage decisions, career decisions, travel decisions, driving decisions, buying decisions, finance decisions, investment decisions. I could write 100 pages on it, but it would be nothing more than a distillation of Kahneman's 781-page book, *Choices, Values and Frames.*

It is big, heavy, brilliant, impenetrable, dense, and makes a great doorstop or a booster seat for your child. Read it.

I contend and will demonstrate in several stories to follow that the difference between one's best interests and one's perceived best interests is where the greatest mismatches occur and where the greatest opportunity to profit exists.

To wit, it was 1995 and I was starting a software company, Atcom Info. But I still maintained a residual passing interest in the real estate racket and was always poking my finger in and around looking for that little crack I could squeeze into, and then like a puff adder blow myself up to twice my size, split apart the rock and see if I could turn the fissure into a couple dollars.

Kraig Kristofferson is a brilliant real estate broker in San Diego. He is marvelous in his own right, but lives somewhat in reflected glory since his brother is Kris Kristofferson, the famous actor and singer. Kraig was a downtown deal guy, and I was always working him for action, information—a deal, a crack in the rock.

One day he comes to me and says there is a building in downtown, a high-rise office building, 287,000 square feet, which is about 65 percent occupied, located across from City Hall. It looked like a classic Senturia deal. It had enough hair on it to make ZZ Top's beard look like a soul patch.

The building in question was the headquarters for Security Pacific Bank. Bank of America had recently bought Security Pacific Bank, the bank itself, and a federal government rule at the time forced B of A to divest itself of a certain percentage of its real estate holdings unless they were occupying the buildings themselves. Under the banking laws, this building did not qualify and therefore, B of A was required to get it off its books.

Rule #212: When the government imposes stupid rules, take advantage of them.

The building had been built in 1974 by Security Pacific Bank to serve as its San Diego headquarters, and since the bank did not want to own the real estate (bad for the balance sheet), it sold the land and building to Mr. Edwin Lowe, with an agreement to lease the building back from him for 40 years. This was a normal and classic sale leaseback bank strategy.

Edwin Lowe was a colorful character, to say the least. He was the inventor of Yahtze, a game he discovered while cruising on a yacht—thus the name. (Don't you just love simple logic? If he had been on a train, the game would have been called "Trainze.")

Lowe was also the inventor of Bingo. He discovered that game while attending a traveling carnival in Atlanta in 1929 where he saw a game being played with dried beans, a rubber numbering stamp, and some cardboard sheets. He brought the game back to New York City where it got some traction. During one of the games, the winner got so excited that instead of yelling out "beano" he blurted out "bingo!" And the rest is history.

I wish I'd had a chance to meet Mr. Lowe, but he died in 1986.

The deal on the table in 1995 had two components: the leasehold (the bank building itself) and the fee (fee is the ownership of the land on which the building sat). And when the term of the master lease expired, the land and building would be joined together again under one ownership, namely the Lowe heirs, whose beneficial interest was being managed by Chase Bank and Trust on behalf of the various family members who, since Bingo's death, had been vigorously feeding at the classic trust fund baby trough.

When I entered the fray, there were these two behemoths, both happily afflicted with arthritis, lethargy, complacency, and the deep desire to do nothing that would in any way either upset their creaming off the steady stream of fees or expose them to claims of malfeasance or stupidity. Say hello to Godzilla meets Megalon.

I rushed into the deal with absolutely imperfect knowledge, assuming that by the time I had to understand what the hell was going on, I would figure it out. My model at that time was simple: sign the deal first, ask questions later.

Rule #339: Not knowing all the facts can prevent you from talking yourself out of the deal before you even get into it. Perfect knowledge leads to perfect paralysis.

Now a key feature of the master lease provided for the owners of the building, represented by Chase, to acquire the master lease if Bank of America accepted a bid from an unrelated third party to step into their shoes and take over their original position.

In other words, if B of A sold their position as master lessee, the boys at Chase would have a period of time in which to match the offer and consolidate the land and the building under one ownership. This would have been very advantageous to Chase and the Lowe heirs, and I assumed that they would box me out of this deal as soon as they got the chance.

Rule #270: Read the fine print. Skimming is fine for Civilization 105, where you read great books of the Western world, but legal documents require a finer comb.

An additional and fascinating feature of the lease provided for the leaseholder, B of A, to recover all the tenant improvement dollars (to amortize those expenses) they had spent before they had to pay Mr. Lowe anything above the very modest base rent.

In 1992, B of A had spent $10 million fixing up the place so they could get the City of San Diego as a tenant. I made my offer in 1995. I don't know if the Chase trustees had ever read the document or not, but to my mind it was a no-brainer.

My game plan was simple. Get my hands on the master lease at any reasonable price, and then I figured the underlying land owner—Chase on behalf of the Lowe heirs—would pay us some money to take our position because it made perfect, logical sense that one would want to consolidate ownership of the land and building, not to mention that the $10 million on the books would go to Chase, and not to the master lessee.

Rule #96: Don't think just because you know what to do, that the other guy will reach the same conclusion. Remember Kahneman's theory about Rational Man Behavior and acting in one's own perceived best self-interest.

When Bingo died, he made the biggest mistake of his life. He allowed a major money center bank to act as trustee on behalf of his estate.

In bold letters, forever indelible, never to be forgotten, I share with you the following.

Rule #9: *Do not ever let a bank act as trustee for your heirs and assignees.*

You would do better to give it all to charity or bury it in the backyard. The inaction, inattention, gross stupidity, greed, and fear of a bank trustee ranks right below manslaughter in the panoply of high crimes and misdemeanors. The word "trustee" is a raging anomaly; a trustee is the last person I would trust.

So let's review the bidding. Chase Bank is the trustee charged with protecting the various Lowe children and wives and ex-wives. The trust is getting payments each year from Security Pacific Bank. Security Pacific gets bought by Bank of America, which assumes the obligation and continues to make payments to Chase, which ostensibly sends the money to the beneficiaries, less some fees.

The building was badly managed and the heirs, who had a participation in cash flow above a certain base floor, were not getting any real dough. The floor was their ceiling, and it wasn't glass; it was concrete, all 23 stories. All they were getting was very modest fixed payments. Remember the first $10 million was being rapidly amortized in favor of B of A, so any chance that came along to consolidate the lease and the fee, nobody in his right mind would pass on that opportunity.

This kind of master lease is sometimes called a sandwich lease. I wanted to be the meat in the middle. The middle guy collects the rent from the tenants (the bottom piece of bread), takes a modest fee for the effort, and then remits to the top piece of bread (Chase) what is left. If you do this correctly, there should be a couple dollars left over, maybe just enough to buy some corn rye bread, Swiss cheese, a kosher dill pickle, sweet hot mustard, and a few slices of Russian pastrami from the Carnegie Deli. In my view there was $10 million of pastrami sitting on the table, right between those two slices of bread.

Enough gastronomy. It was the classic find-a-crack in the great wall of banking and egos and long distance (Chase and the heirs were in New York City) and see if I could stick a finger in there and crumb out a few pieces of gold.

So I made an offer to buy the master lease position. I think the offer was $250,000. Once again, I did not exactly have all the money in the bank ready to go at the time of the offer, but I figured that by the time I had to close, I would have raced around as usual and found a couple of friendly chuckleheads to join me.

But there was another minor treble hook out there. It was not just the money for the deal that I needed. I also had to demonstrate "capacity." Capacity meant that I had to look like Bank of America. The security for the stream of payments being paid to Chase was backed by the stature and capacity of the largest bank in the world. And I was supposed to give comfort to Chase in that very special way: I am there for you, baby.

I did not need to demonstrate billions, but I needed to appear to have "substantial capacity," just in case the rents failed to meet the required payment stream.

And as if that weren't enough hair, there was one more minor fishhook, more like a grappling hook, in the lease. It said that if B of A accepted an offer, then Chase had 20 days to match the offer, blow us out of the water, step into our shoes on the same terms and conditions, and become the purchaser of the lease. Only an idiot bank trustee would not act timely to take over the lease and consolidate the ownership.

B of A accepted our offer and the notice was duly sent (registered return receipt requested) to the boys at Chase, exactly as required. I waited.

I waited.

Rule #316: Time actually does slow down when you are waiting for it to run out. Consider the final minutes of any sporting event. I call this Stephen Hawking meets the shot at the buzzer or, as Einstein once famously said, "Time slows down as speed increases."

And then the deadline passed. I had the deal "tied up."

Literally 48 hours after the deadline had passed, the boys in New York woke up screaming for a second chance. They wanted a breakfast ball.

NFW.

The Bible says God rested on the seventh day. Maybe so, but his lawyers didn't. Within a week Chase sued me.

They had a raft of claims, but a primary one was that my offer was not a bona fide offer, since I was a small time pisher with no capacity. And while they were at it, they threw in a few other insults. A good lawyer throws the book; these guys threw the entire library.

But the irrefutable fact was this: The 20 days had passed. The true tale will never be known, but somewhere in the dark bowels of Chase Bank there was a nice, well-meaning employee (man or woman, who knows) who must have been asleep or on vacation or bored or whatever. This person never got around to opening the registered letter notifying them that the time period had begun—until the time period had expired. It just got mistook, misplaced, misunderstood, mislaid, misguided—just missed.

A bank trustee abhors change. He prefers not to have to make a decision. After all, put yourself in his shoes. Here he was, sitting in nice offices on the 53rd floor of a Manhattan glass-and-steel high-rise, clipping coupons, and some short, wild man in San Diego lobs a firebomb in the window, trying to blow him out of the water.

Humpty Dumpty, pal.

The bank trustee mantra is the powerful prayer: "Dear God, let me cover my ass and keep my job. And while I have your ear, dear God, please keep those fees rolling in."

The lawsuit arrived and among the many things they accused me of, one was that I had no capacity. In other words, I was a pisher with no standing. Go away, little boy. Where had I heard that before? Moi, no capacity? Hey asshole, you want capacity? I'll give you capacity.

So I went looking for some big motherfuckers who might be wandering along through the valley of the shadow of death and wanted a deal.

And I found three of them. One of them was my old friend, Michael Moers, who by now was out of prison and back in the real estate business—bigger, badder, richer, and smarter than ever. The second caballero was Rick Wolfen. He was like the guy in a David Mamet heist movie, the one who is detailed, organized, thorough, meticulous, and makes sure the rest of the gang doesn't leave their fingerprints on the gun. The third guy ran a hedge fund, had a monster balance sheet, lived in New York, and I never met him.

Capacity? Bring it on!

Rule #293: "We're putting the band back together." —Jake Blues, *The Blues Brothers*

The four of us became equal partners in a war of litigation that might bankrupt us if we lost and might bankrupt us if we won. Litigation is like watching grass grow while you water the lawn with hundred dollar bills. But there always comes a time, usually late in the game, when you have a chance to break out the John Deere 25-horsepower twin-blade giant-ass mower and do some serious cutting. It is at that time that Rational Man Behavior needs to be strenuously embraced.

I will not bore you with the 2 ½ years of litigation and maneuvering that followed. Both banks waged war against us and against each other. There were a plethora of claims and counter-claims, but this is not a book on legal litigation theory.

Rule #300: It never hurts to ask.

At the beginning of the litigation, we had won one key point. We felt we were bona fide and entitled to our bargain, and as such, we had argued to the B of A lawyer, that were we to win, we should be entitled to maintain our position. And as such, at the least, the excess income, above the basic building expenses, should be escrowed. They agreed. In other words, the basic bills got paid, but there were no distributions to the Chase gang. It was a standstill agreement until the case was resolved. But there was no wiggle room. It was winner take all.

Finally, after the scorched-earth salvos of shit-slinging had subsided, the three parties agree to settle. We had won the fair lady. Everyone flies out to San Diego and the closing takes place in a conference room like the one in *The Hudsucker Proxy*—big. It has your basic 35-foot- long marble table, and up and down each side were stacks of documents with little red, yellow, and green tabs indicating where to sign.

Rick Wolfen and I were representing our side, along with our attorney, Brian Seltzer. The two banks had nine lawyers and principals wandering around the room. We were polite and unassuming. After all, no need to be arrogant pricks. We had beaten the giants;

we were the winners. (Check out *Bull Durham* to learn how to behave when arriving at the Show.)

There was some polite chitchat at the outset, but at best it had been a war of attrition and we just wanted to sign and get the fuck out of Dodge.

The basic terms had the four partners paying Chase $725,000, plus another $300,000 in legal fees. We were to pay Bank of America $900,000 for agreeing to certain clauses. And we owed another $900,000 in commissions and fees. It looked like we were finally going to get to eat that pastrami sandwich. There was roughly $2.8 million about to be chopped up, distributed, shuffled, sliced, diced, and swirled around the table, and everyone was looking to us for their cut. No problem, I'm there for you, baby. Get out the Mont Blanc, I'm ready.

Right then, the lead lawyer for Chase takes center stage and begins to expostulate with some legal mumbo jumbo yadda yadda, and then like a fucking terrorist, he opens up his jacket and strapped to his chest is 40 pounds of dynamite. He says, ". . . and so in conclusion, there is no deal unless you pay us another $150,000." QED meets IED.

Huh!? What the fuck! We had a deal.

I say, "You're coming in here at the 11th hour and 57th minute, putting a gun to our heads, using extortion and threatening to blow the deal unless we chip in another 150 grand. Is that what you're doing?"

"Yes."

You gotta admire the guy's candor. Very, very, very large *cojones*.

And at that moment, my beloved partner, Rick Wolfen, loses it. He goes ballistic. Words like "asshole," "scumbag," and "cocksucker" seem to be bouncing off the walls. Not to mention "dishonest," "dishonorable," and that favorite of the BP saga, "shakedown."

Houston, we have a problem.

Mr. Wolfen, normally the model of probity and discretion, is apoplectic and stalks out of the conference room, hurling a final, nuanced suggestion: "See you in court, motherfucker."

He is out of there. I turn to the assembled group of bank lawyers and tell them, "Nothing serious, gentlemen. Let's take a short time-out."

I race into the lobby, grab Rick, and hustle him into the men's room, followed closely by Seltzer.

Rick begins to slowly relax, but he is clearly still outraged. He argues for calling the guy's bluff. Do not pay, do not settle, press on, finish the lawsuit. We will be vindicated in the courtroom.

Remember Rule #195 at the start of the chapter. You can defer legal fees but you cannot avoid them.

Well, the third guy in the men's room was our lawyer.

"Rick," I say, "we owe Mr. Seltzer about $746,000 in legal fees. We have paid $300,000 to date. So if we walk out of this settlement and do not take the deal, including the insult, I am sure Brian will continue to wage war on our behalf, but I suspect he will request his fees be brought a bit more current."

Brian was helpful here. He simply said, "Yes."

How can you not love the clarity of self-benefit analysis? Imagine a lawyer wanting to be paid. The idea is revolutionary.

"So Rick, my dearest partner, where in the fuck are we going to come up with another $446,000 just for legal fees to get current and then another X hundred thousand to continue to wage a new war?"

And so I pointed out to Rick that Rational Man Behavior (acting in one's properly perceived true best self-interest) was to suck it up and settle. We all lamented the miserable behavior of the lawyer in question, but this was the classic time to bite our collective tongue. After all, the market had improved and the occupancy of the building had even increased a little.

So I left Wolfen in the men's room and returned to the conference room alone, where the other side was smirking. No one likes smirkers.

And I delivered the following modest commentary:

"Ladies and gentlemen, while I do not think your request is a reasonable one, and clearly borders on extortion, nonetheless, we have given careful consideration to all the issues and are delighted to pay Chase the additional requested compensation and close. Give me the fucking pen and let's sign and be done."

Which we all did.

Rule #285: Never stand on principle when a ladder is available.

We owed $2.8 million and with the added insult of $150,000, we were up to $2.95 million cash on the barrelhead. But, as you may remember, B of A had agreed to escrow the rent money during the legal war. The war had lasted 2 ½ years, and at the close of the deal, we assumed the master lease. Along with that obligation came the dough that had been accumulating in escrow. And it belonged to us. And would you believe, funny you should mention it, that number came to exactly $3 million.

Think about it. Essentially we paid these shitheels with their own money. You gotta love America.

The four of us paid Seltzer's legal fees, and we were now the proud owners of a very large pastrami sandwich.

Rule #5: The wheel is always spinning.

Now, to fully amplify and detail this rule would take another entire book, but let it suffice that this is one rule that must never be forgotten. Ever!

Allow me to illustrate.

For three weeks after the signing, there was the usual post-closing crap. The lawyers for Chase and B of A prepared and collated the closing binder, filed and recorded a variety of legalese, and of course they double-checked all the documents and signatures.

And then Brian gets a call from one of the Chase attorneys, who says, "Blah blah yadda yadda yadda, in our review of the documents, we found a minor mistake, a misprint, actually. It seems that we left off a zero in paragraph 23 of the whatever document, and we both know that the clause should actually refer back to the number in paragraph 22 yadda yadda, and since we all knew what it was supposed to be and since it was just an honest mistake that we made, we will be sending you a revised page for your clients to sign."

Huh.

"Well, yes, Brian, it is true that we did prepare the documents. But it was just a simple mistake, and all the parties knew what was intended and we need to correct this, because if we don't, it means a substantial financial loss to my clients, which certainly is not fair, is it?"

Huh.

"Brian, it was a minor misprint, we all knew what it was sup-posed to be, and frankly, I need to fix this little problem, because it is not going to be good for my legal career to have Chase suffer a financial loss of this magnitude, simply because of a minor draft-ing error. I am sure your clients know what is intended and would be more than willing to sign the revised page."

Brian replied, "Well, that is an interesting problem you've got there. I will discuss it with my client."

Brian called and explained the issue and the request.

"You're telling me that the same shitheel law firm that just stuck a $150,000 watermelon up my ass now wants me to do what? Re-sign something, agree to something that was their mistake, do the right thing, cover their ass, put a band-aid on that exposed, puss-filled wound so his daddy will not be angry with him and ground him permanently? Tell him to die and pound sand."

As you can see, I really did not have strong feelings on the mat-ter. Nor did my wonderful partner, Mr. Wolfen, who concurred word for word.

And how much money was involved in this little misplaced paragraph and misapplied journal ledger entry?

Yup—$150,000.

Final addendum: From 1998 through 2014, when the master lease on the building will finally expire, our partnership (the four pishers without capacity) will have taken out a total of $13.9 million—net to us.

Now that's what I call a Carnegie Deli pastrami sandwich!

CHAPTER 7

RENEGOTIATION IS WHAT HAPPENS WHEN THE DEAL YOU THINK YOU THOUGHT YOU MADE TURNS OUT TO BE THE DEAL THAT THE OTHER SIDE DIDN'T THINK THEY THOUGHT THEY WOULD HAVE EVER MADE IF THEY HAD KNOWN THEN WHAT THEY KNOW NOW

Rule #238: If you play tennis with yourself, you can never serve an ace.

If you always know how the other guy is going to react, how the other person is going to think, what the other person is going to say, you have a reasonably high chance of failure.

It's like playing tennis against yourself: Since you know where you are going to hit the ball, you would go there, in which case you wouldn't hit it there, you would hit it somewhere else, but since you know where that would be also, you can't hit it there either. And eventually, as you can see, you would never even hit the ball because there is no place you do not know where you are going hit it. And given perfect knowledge, you would never even get out on the court.

You can be so smart that you negotiate yourself right out of the deal.

Since you know what you would say if you were on the other side of a transaction, you often assume (wrongly) that the other guy is just as smart as you are, and thus he would never agree to the terms you are proposing.

So, you never propose terms highly favorable to yourself, since you know of course that you would never accept those terms. If you already know the outcome of the game, there is no point in even opening the can of balls.

Rule #362: You can't know what the other guy is going to say until you give him a chance to say it, and you can't give him a chance to say it unless you ask—and then shut up and wait.

Rule #363: It never hurts to ask, as long as you do it politely and in a soft tone of voice.

It is 1989, and there is an interesting piece of land downtown, known as the T.M. Cobb block. Cobb made wooden doors and windows, and his factory was in the middle of the redevelopment zone, and again this piece of land was situated across the street from what was going to become the new convention center.

Rule #298: Time and timing matter.

This is one of the 10 rules that are absolutely inviolate. Please feel free to list the 234,818,099 examples in your own life where this axiom has been true. (Start with your birth.)

A real estate broker had become aware that Mr. Cobb was going to sell his land and he called me. I was advised that Mr. Cobb already had an offer on the table and was going to sign it that afternoon. I had coveted this piece of land for a couple years and had actually met with Mr. Cobb once to indicate my desire. He had politely shooed me away. At that time he was not a seller. But now that he was, it looked like I was going to be too late to the dance.

The broker told me what he thought the price and terms were: $88 per square foot with a fairly long escrow.

Always remember Rule #298, especially when you see the woman you want to marry getting on a subway going in the opposite direction.

I was in Los Angeles that day, when I learned of this opportunity, so I immediately drove to San Diego that afternoon, got in to see Mr. Cobb at 5 p.m., and handed him a non-refundable check, no contingencies, for $100,000, a price of $92 per square foot. The deal was mine.

I had won. Well, that depends again on how you define winning. What I had actually won was the right to wage war for 11 more years. It must be obvious by now that my idea of winning is less than traditional. This comes under the heading of be careful what you wish for, you may get it.

This piece of land was at the foot of Fifth Avenue in the sacred and historical Gaslamp District. There existed architectural and contextual and historical and height rules and overlays governing this piece of land, but hey, I had an idea that what San Diego needed was architectural greatness and a bold vision.

Rule #127: Get a new pair of glasses, or Lasik.

I proposed a contemporary high-rise condominium tower. By this time, the One Harbor Drive towers (the Bruce Stark deal) were under construction, the real estate recession had not yet arrived in full force, and I thought the town was ready for the famous architect Frank Gehry. I met with Gehry in Los Angeles, but this project was not his cup of tea. If you can't get Frank, then the next stop if you want to blow the doors off is Arquitectonica, a Miami firm right out of Don Johnson, *Miami Vice*, red Ferrari, wrap-around shades, pastel shirt open to the waist, baby, light my fire.

Bold, famous, outrageous, and iconic, this firm was best known for a condo project that was built with a hole in the middle. You could fly a Cessna through the center of the building. Bright colors, big design—what critics might call "out on the edge" and "pushing the boundaries."

I was going to bring big-time, bold, iconic, world-class, ego-driven insanity to this little burg and show the petite functionaries with their pedestrian rules and community plan and historical district and integrated into the fine-grained fabric of the street vision that San Diego was ready to be put on the map with a big architectural statement.

Rule #390: *Are you out of your fucking mind?*

Bernardo Fort-Brescia and his wife, Laurinda Spear, the two principals of the firm, came to San Diego to discuss the project, and we agreed to go forward. At this point, I did not have any partners yet, so I was fronting the pre-development dough myself.

Rule #271: High-risk insanity may cause damage to your marriage.

You had not even finished one high-rise and you were up to your ass in another one. Do you like catching knives while blindfolded?

By this time, I had been married for nine years to Deborah, my lovely second wife, and we had two children, and I thought we were happy. But to Deborah's way of thinking, my career lifestyle choices seemed to her more like she had married a Las Vegas gambling addict rather than a solid, middle-class, respectable, nice Jewish boy, which her father had previously indicated would have been his first choice.

Nota bene: By this time, one of his three daughters had gotten divorced from the suitable doctor, so Bernie, the father, was now only batting .500, while my game still had runners on base.

I was on a roll, and so I hired Bernardo and Laurinda to break every rule in the master plan, historic, Gaslamp overlay zone. And I got what I paid for. It was glass and steel and dynamic and looked like the painter Mondrian had come to San Diego and had an epileptic fit. It was spectacular.

And I floated this bold balloon to the powers that be. And it pissed off every person on CCDC, as well as the entire City

Council and five different downtown organizations that had quasi-jurisdiction over my piece of dirt. They emphatically said no, drop dead, go fuck yourself, you are out of your mind, it is never going to happen, you can take your New York City avant-garde sensibility and modern architecture pretensions and deep-six them off Point Loma, pal.

Rule #225: Can you spell self-destructive?

Bernardo himself made the presentation in front of the planning committee in charge of approvals. This world-famous architect unveiled his vision, but when he got back on the plane that afternoon, he handed me a final bill and a handwritten note that said, "Never going to happen in this town, good bye and good luck."

So now I had a bit of a problem. I was whipping through my own dough, did not have any approvals, nor any likelihood of approvals and did not have any partners. The usual story, a fight for love and glory. I was getting a bit concerned.

Once again, however, Elijah showed up at the door, this time in the form of one Jeremy Cohen from the S.D. Malkin Company, a major big-time condominium developer from New York City. And of course, just by coincidence, they were looking for a project in San Diego. So what else is new?

And just as I had done with Mr. Stark, I convinced Mr. Cohen and his boss, Scott Malkin, that I am there for you, baby.

Nota bene: Scott Malkin is the son of Peter Malkin, who is one of the partners who own the ground lease on the Empire State Building. This family was definitely New York City real estate royalty.

Scott was following in the footsteps of his father, and his most trusted foot soldier was Jeremy Cohen, sent out to the hinterlands of San Diego to check out this golden opportunity.

Jeremy had an education from Harvard, had been with Malkin for several years, and was a trained real estate developer with an amazing sense of design. This guy was the real deal: a talent who could maybe save my ass.

We liked each other, and in particular, Jeremy liked that this was a project that he could guide, that he could drive, that he could shape, on which he could be the numero uno, the prime creator for its success, thus getting out from under the thumb of Scott in New York. New territory and a free hand for greatness.

Rule #245: All deals get made for more than one reason. Find the other one—that is the one that will drive the deal.

Jeremy wanted freedom, and I had just what he craved: a great location, a totally blank slate (since my first two designs had been soundly rejected; a second attempt was "too bulky," they said), and I was willing to sit in the back seat. Cohen liked to drive. If need be, I would have ridden in the trunk.

And he had one more spectacular thing going for him—deep pockets.

Rule #92: If you are the richest guy at the table, find another table.

And so we began. The deal was simple. They put up all the dough going forward (the $246,000 I had already pissed away stayed in the deal), and I got a carried 25 percent interest with no penalties and no offsets.

After about 18 months of waging war with the same agencies, planning groups, committees, and gadflies that had told me to die and pound sand, the real estate market crashed and a mid-rise condominium was not going to pencil in that location, and a high-rise was never going to be approved. In addition, the escrow period had already been extended a couple times, and we had to finally close on the land and pay Mr. Cobb.

And so old man Cobb took his dough and laughed all the way to San Diego Trust and Savings Bank.

Things were not going well. The deal made no sense as residential. We would have to try something else. What's left? Oh, of course. Wouldn't it be fun to build a hotel?

Huh.

Well, all bets are off now, and Cohen comes to me and says, "Look, Neil, we made our deal with you based on certain assumptions and representations, and frankly, not one of them has come to pass so we feel that the deal we made is not exactly the deal we would have made if we had known what we didn't know. Now that we do know what we do know, and given all the issues and feelings, let me put it to you in a delicate, sensitive, reasonable way: *We want to re-negotiate.*"

Rule #205: Always be willing to renegotiate.

On the face of it, this rule might seem a bit strange, even counter-intuitive. After all, the original deal I had made was pretty favorable to me. Now, I play golf with a lawyer, a sweet, marvelous guy, but he will never renegotiate on the golf course. You know, if the teams are unfair after nine holes, he will never allow the bet or the handicaps to be revised. He says, "A deal's a deal."

I hate this part of him, but look, he's a lawyer so I forgive him. You always renegotiate, and I will tell you why.

Rule #318: Because renegotiating is the right thing to do.

If the deal is terribly unfair, it will never stick. And you will be in either litigation or the crapper before the whole thing is over. You can't make someone commit suicide. Even if you are sure you will never, ever, ever see this person again, no way, no how, never— still remember this: The wheel is always spinning. And your paths will cross again. They always do.

Now I know that the big-time deal boys, when they have the upper hand, they do not renegotiate. Their preferred method of operation is to put their foot on your neck and press. Never give up an advantage.

I simply do not think that way. Right or wrong, it just isn't my style.

So Jeremy comes to me and says, look we are now into this dog for $700,000-plus, and there appears to be no way out, except to make a 180-degree turn and develop a hotel on the site, and that means more money from us and more time and more risk, and the deal you made is too good for you and not good enough for us, so let's sit down and talk.

I actually felt bad for the boys from New York. After all, I had now become friends with Jeremy, a real friendship, and I did not have many friends. I had 309 acquaintances. I knew everybody in town, but I was pretty guarded on the friend front.

Let's review the bidding. The Malkin team had relied on what I had promised to deliver, and while there were certainly extenuating circumstances (which is code for "It's not all my fault!"), nonetheless they certainly had not gotten their bargain. Everything they had counted on had turned to shit, so fair is fair, step up and take your medicine.

Rule #333: God occasionally gives you a chance to do a mitzvah or be a mensch. Never pass up any of these opportunities.

And so we renegotiated. And the boys from New York were tough. The new deal was byzantine. There were multiple tranches of debt and equity along with various mezzanine financing look-back recalculations. There were tiered interest rates and water-falls, tied to when the project got started, got finished, what it cost, what it might sell for, along with a few what-if-it-rains-in-Poughkeepsie-in-Novembers. There was one point in the nego-tiation where it was so complicated and convoluted that Cohen himself could not understand what the lawyer had written, and Cohen was the one who had dictated the deal to him. I just got my raincoat and hung on.

I was still in the deal in some fashion, but it would take a full lunar eclipse (next scheduled for 2008) coupled with an overly exu-berant, booming real estate market before I would ever see any of my money back—let alone a profit.

But I did get one concession: After they got back all their pref-erences and all of their back-carried interest and all of their costs and all their look-backs, and after we paid back the mortgage and the cost of anything and everything that could be charged to this project, then and only then, I would get 25 percent of what was left.

The offer they made was simple. I got to ride in the back seat, keep my mouth shut, stay out of trouble, let Cohen drive the bus, and when the whole thing was over, I would get 25 percent of whatever was left after all the bones had been picked clean. Like a waiter clearing the table and cadging the last lamb chop left on the plate as he goes back to the kitchen.

At that same time, my wife, Ms. Deborah, said she could no longer take our lifestyle. She called it "gambling." I called it investing. The constant up and down, the always raising money, the political approvals and denials, the constant risk of totally going broke—it made her crazy. She headed for the door with a goodbye and good luck and my lawyer will call your lawyer.

Not a lot of choices. By Jeremy's calculation, the hotel would have to sell for over $65 million for me to ever see a dime. He figured that event was so unlikely that it was better for the Malkin side to get all the interest and preferences rather than a bigger percentage at the back-end. There wasn't going to be any back-end, to their way of thinking.

No cards, so the right answer is, I am there for you, baby. I accepted their proposal. But I got to feel good about myself. I had done the right thing by my partners. They wanted to hedge their bets and cut their risk and I agreed to let them do that by changing the deal and putting myself in a worse position. And anyway, it was clear that for the next few years I was going to be a bit consumed with that thing called divorce.

The Cobb war story goes on for eight more years. Cohen finally finished the hotel in June 2000. It was gorgeous, and it won dozens of design awards. (Jeremy is a monster talent.) It became a Hilton flag property and was a huge success.

Rule #85: Don't be greedy.

OK, this is a very basic rule. But you would be surprised how often it is ignored. Something happens when money shows up; people seem to get very confused very quickly.

It was 2004 and that lunar eclipse was due in a few years. The real estate market was "frothy," and I suggested to Jeremy that now would be a wonderful time to sell the hotel.

But, the boys from New York said, "No." There were more ups in the deal, hang on.

"Huh. Are you out of your minds? The market is nuts; let's unload this dog."

Rule #306: Bad decisions often come from places that are not easy to see until you pull back the covers and look at whose horse head is in the bed.

Malkin and Cohen were getting fees. If we sold the hotel, those would dry up. But to their credit, Rational Man Behavior finally took hold, and they agreed to at least sell just the hotel and hang on to the ground floor retail (so there would still be some fees).

In January 2005, we flipped this baby to LaSalle Hotel Properties—just the 282-room hotel, not the retail, for $85 million. That was a lot more money than anyone had ever contemplated in 1993 when we renegotiated. Even after the tranched waterfalls, mezzanine geysers, and preferred interest rate fountains, no matter how you spray it, that was a Niagara Falls of money.

You do the math. My act of contrition, remorse, and decency had just netted me over $5 million.

This deal had more twists, switchbacks, spins, maneuvers, and blind curves than the North Yungas Road that connects Coroico to La Paz in Bolivia (affectionately known as the road of death).

CHAPTER 8

BE RESPECTFUL OF INVESTORS

(THEIR MONEY DID NOT GROW ON TREES)

Lots of people who never finished high school are in the top 1 percent of wealth in America (IQ and net worth have no correlation). The point I want to make—vigorously—is that when interacting with rich people, it is usually safe to assume that they are smart in some Rational Man Behavior significant way. Maybe they are dumb-like-a-fox smart or street smart or Mensa smart or seat-of-the-pants smart, but they are serious men and women when it comes to money. These are people who have built fortunes on everything from brooms to burgers to balloons, and if you want to pitch them to raise money, you should assume they will figure it out, maybe later rather than sooner, but they are not sheep to the slaughter. And as such, proper care and feeding of the angel investor is necessary.

Rule #111: Don't offer evil, rapacious, stupid terms to your angel investors, even if you can get away with it. That kind of deal structure will come back to haunt you.

You need a little background here. For most entrepreneurs, the ones who need to rely on family, friends, and fools, the toughest part of the deal is not the technology or the product, it is the financial structure, and along with that comes their overwhelming and unreasonable fear of the D word. Dilution.

Rule #28: Dilution is relatively meaningless. Which would you rather own: .023 percent of Google or 89 percent of Walt's Pizza Parlor in Lemon Grove, California?

When I ask my graduate students at SDSU this question, 100 percent of them get it right. But I can tell you from concrete evidence that when they are sitting across the table from a real investor and they are trying to make the deal, most of them will get it wrong.

In the abstract, they always understand about the size of the pie versus the size of the slice, but when they get up close and personal, they drop the ball and the pizza 50 percent of the time.

Let's suppose you want to finance a new venture. It doesn't matter if it is a lemonade stand, a restaurant, or a high-tech, solar, bio-fuel plant. At some point, you are going to need to raise some money. And the normal initial route is the 3 Fs: friends, family, and fools.

The three Fs are not usually investment professionals. They are considering the deal for a multitude of disparate reasons, they want to help you or they believe in you. They would like to make some money also. (In many cases, they simply want to get their money back.)

If it is a parent/uncle, he says to himself: I'll never see the money again, and what the hell it just reduces whatever inheritance little Harry was going to get anyway, so I will give him a chance now.

If it is a friend, he says: I would like to get the money back, I am willing to invest, I really don't know what the proper and fair deal should be so I will trust Harry to do the right thing.

If it is a fool, then more so than either of the above, you, the entrepreneur, have the affirmative obligation to treat him better than he would know how to treat himself.

Rule #206: When you have the upper hand with more perfect knowledge and you are negotiating with someone less skilled than you in the art of finance, then it is incumbent, it is required, it is absolute that you must negotiate for him and actually make the deal better than he would have made on his own.

Do not argue with me on this one. Trust me. The wheel is always spinning, and when it comes time to settle up or raise more money, previously ill-conceived behavior in this area will rip your heart out and potentially destroy your deal.

I take this rule to heart vigorously. I believe in it deeply and I try to live by it.

However, let me elaborate some nuances.

In the case of Bruce Stark, for example, it was a fair fight. He was not a friend, nor was he a fool. He was a very sophisticated, very wealthy, very experienced player in the real estate field, so in my negotiations with him, every tactic and every advantage, psychological or legal, was fair and should be taken.

However, if I were seeking money from Bruce Stark for a software technology, medical device company, where clearly he is not an expert, where the terms "broad-based weighted average anti-dilution and liquidated preferences" do not roll trippingly roll off his tongue, then it is my obligation to treat him more than fairly because I am more armed in that space than he is.

When you take money from your high school chum who made his fortune in raincoats and galoshes, and if you ever wish to speak with him again, you need to bend over backwards to make it fair, to give him a fighting chance to make a return on his investment.

I see this syndrome repeatedly from young entrepreneurs who come to me for money and when I ask to see the cap table—the capital structure of the previous financing—and they tell me proudly that they were able to only give away 3 percent of the company for $300,000—they have put themselves and their investor in a very black box, the kind Penn and Teller saw in half.

The risk of the first round of financing is not thinking about the next round of financing.

Let's analyze this a bit more closely.

Young Bobby, the entrepreneur, convinces his Uncle Lucius back his scheme without thinking through what will happen when young Bobby needs more money from a professional investor. Uncle Lucius was going to leave Bobby some money in his will anyway, but he wouldn't know a pre-money valuation from a CD-ROM. Still, he says to himself, hey, he's my nephew. So he writes the check for $300,000 and receives 300,000 shares at $1 each.

The deal structure that Bobby has created values the company at $10 million post-money. (Calculation is 3% X 10M = $300,000.) Now you remember the rule that says you need to love and nurture investors, especially friends, family, and fools. And the corollary rule is when you know more than the other guy, you need to act not only in your own best self-interest, but his as well. You need to protect the naïf.

If you do not do that, here is the risk:

In a few months, young Bobby finds that he is close to getting his product out the door, but he needs just a little more cash.

He comes to see me. My opinion of his quarter-baked scheme is based on hard numbers and a strong grasp of the market opportunity as well as the cost to get to break-even, his customers, the team and, believe me, my valuation of his company is definitely going to be less than the hope, puffery, and fantasy he sold to Uncle Lucius.

Young Bobby needs $500,000 more to complete the product and get to market. I tell him I am inclined to invest that amount at a pre-money valuation of $2M.

I agree to invest $500,000 at a valuation of $2 million. That means that after the financing closes, I own one-fifth (500,000 divided by 2.5 million) or 20 percent of the company on a fully diluted basis. Now remember that Uncle Lucius paid one dollar per share for his stock, and I have just paid 20 cents per share for my stock.

What happens to the favorite Uncle Lucius, who used to take Bobby to the zoo? He is going to be standing in his galoshes up to his neck in a force five hurricane. He goes from owning 3 percent of the company for his $300,000 to now owning approximately 2.3 percent. However, the issue is not ownership, the issue is price. And his $300,000 is now worth $60,000. (Calculation: 300,000 shares X the current price of 20 cents.)

Young Bobby has just fed Uncle Lucius to the lions.

And you know what happens next. Uncle Lucius bites his tongue and tells his nephew that he still loves him and wishes him good luck. Then he calls up his estate attorney and writes the dumb son of a bitch nephew out of the will for taking advantage of him.

The kid loses a few million dollars of inheritance in exchange for a short-lived fantasy not to suffer serious dilution. See you at the reading of the will, pal.

Rule #288: The issue of fair negotiation is even more important when hiring employees.

Even if you have the upper hand (it is a tough job market), you need to remember that the wheel is always spinning. And what you don't want to do is hire someone, teach them the business, take advantage of them, have them feel abused, get fed up and leave you, and then go to your competition directly across the street. Happens all the time.

Rule #229: The value of your company lies primarily in the workforce. Nothing more need be said about this rule. It is obvious.

And to finish my last thoughts on rich and stupid, leaving aside trust fund babies and lottery winners, the wealthy among us got there not only with brains but with other qualities such as tenacity, vision, persistence, courage, and fierce commitment. Those are qualities that are powerful and that any entrepreneur should seek to find and internalize. You may think your investor is a bit of a hayseed, but remember he owns a 126,000-acre farm—and sometime later in the deal you may need some cattle.

CHAPTER 9

"I FEEL YOUR PAIN"

(BILL CLINTON)

Rule #59: Negotiating is like riding a bike. Everyone can do it at some level. And then there is Lance Armstrong.

I have spent 60 years negotiating. I started with my parents as soon as I could talk, and I am still at it, including a stint with the electrician last week and the refinance mortgage broker this week. Next week there will be new opportunities to move the ball around. Negotiating is the same as breathing. It is a 24/7 pursuit of oxygen and excellence.

There are 179 books on how to negotiate, from "win-win" to "burn the motherfuckers at the stake." After years of experience and reading these books, I have come to one compelling conclusion about the subject.

Rule #11: Persuaders give reasons. Negotiators give concessions.

We all have been in situations where the other side wants to give the reasons why their perspective is clear, rational, reasonable, in everyone's best interests, and should be adopted. This person is trying to persuade.

"You dumb shit, why can't you see that I am right? I have given you 23 reasons why, I have explained what is so obvious to everyone but you. Why can't you see it my way, which I might add, is the correct way?"

These people assume that they can persuade me with their reasons. And when I say, "No, I don't want to do that," they come back and give me some more reasons. They are under the mistaken impression that if they give their reasons a third or fourth time to make sure that I really do understand their reasons, then somehow that will convince me to agree.

"The reason you should sell me the house for $490,000 is because the roof leaks, the street is noisy, the kitchen is old, there are only two bedrooms, and the hillside is prone to geologic movement."

"You know, Betty, I understand your reasons and why you think that because of those reasons the house is only worth $490,000 but I would like to sell it to you for $530,000."

"What is your reasoning? I have explained to you why your house is only worth $490,000."

"My reason is that I don't want to sell for $490,000."

"But that is not a reason."

"No, Betty, in fact, that is my good reason. The reason is I don't want to. I am hopeful and almost believe that I might get an offer next week from a man who only needs one bedroom and is a structural engineer, who is not concerned about the earth movement, and who, by the way, just by chance, has a wife who likes to renovate kitchens as a hobby."

I might also add, "Betty, I feel your reasons. I identify with your reasons, I understand your reasons and I know, from your perspective, that those are all good reasons. But the reason I want to sell for $530,000 is that I think the house is worth it, and $490,000 is not enough money for me to get my motor boat fixed."

Rule #257: Behind all the stated reasons is usually a real reason and a real motive.

So you can see that now there is a chance for a deal, especially if the buyer happens to have a friend who owns the Mercury outboard franchise in the city.

Rule #451: "Give me a long enough lever and a place to stand and I can move the world." —Archimedes

The corollary is: "You pick the price, I pick the terms." —Senturia

The key to a successful negotiation is not to keep repeating the reasons. The key is to listen and give concessions. And in giving concessions, there are a few key principles.

1. Make sure the other side really knows that it is a concession. You can't just toss something in. It has to have real value to the other side. Throwing in the priceless Old Spode soup tureen your mother brought with her from Russia in 1921 is probably not going to get you there if the other side eats off plastic plates.

2. The first concession needs to be the biggest one. After that, go for the slow play. Grind. Give each concession reluctantly. Less and less, more begrudgingly.

3. Make them work for each concession. No freebies. Do not concede too easily. Women have been teaching men this rule since the cave man. Learn from your ancestors.

The above is one school of thought. It is not the only school of thought.

There is a second school of thought. It says cut to the chase, make all the concessions you would have made at one time and then say, "Here is the deal, take it or leave it." And mean it.

They are both excellent. They both work. It depends on your opponent.

Rule #97: One size does not fit all, even in condoms. Measure the other side carefully. It matters.

I have a business partner, Jeremy Cohen. I have mentioned him earlier in connection with the Cobb/Hilton project. Jeremy loves to negotiate. He is of the first school. He likes the foreplay, the dance. He wants to enjoy the whole evening. He doesn't want it to end too quickly. There are so many things to discuss, to debate, so many nuances and possibilities. He enjoys each glorious detail, and no issue is too easily resolved because each issue has multiple scenarios and "What ifs?" and there is always the "in the event that" or "just in case." He loves the process. He is a highly trained Orthodox Jew, comfortable in parsing the Torah and Haftorah's every word, each with multiple meanings, depending on context. It is his nature. And he is very good at his game.

On the other hand, I also love the game. But I am more of the Roger Federer School of Negotiation. Serve, short rally, hit the passing shot, next point.

You can graduate from either school. Just remember: Don't give me reasons, give me concessions. And when all else fails, try something simple like, "That just doesn't work for me." And then shut up, say nothing more. Stop.

Rule #253: Silence is a powerful negotiating tool.

"No, no, don't speak. Don't speak. Please don't speak. No, no, no." —Helen Sinclair, *Bullets over Broadway*

Need I say more?

Rule #66: "Make me an offer" is a reasonable response to almost everything (except when your wife asks you to take out the trash).

The issue worth examining is why it is so difficult for so many people to say that phrase.

Rule #79: The only thing worse than not getting what you want is getting what you want and not knowing it.

I think that is why the process of negotiation is so difficult for many of us. If you ask for a proposal, and you get one, then you are forced to confront what it is you really want. And that goes back to Kahneman and Rational Man Behavior and acting in what is your own best-perceived self-interest.

And being confronted with having to know what you want, should want, might want, might be worthy of, might not be entitled to—all of that is so sufficiently daunting that for many of us, it is simply easier not to ask. If I don't know what I don't have, then at least I am not unhappy about knowing what I didn't get because after all it was never offered, because—you guessed it —I never asked.

And I never asked because it might be perceived as over-reaching or greedy or stupid and then I might be rejected, and I don't like being rejected, so if I don't ask, I can't get hurt, so the truth is I am better off with the bowl of porridge than the marbled New York strip steak, which, after all, I don't really deserve, and besides, steak is not easy to digest and my mother always overcooked the meat anyway because she was always so concerned with salmonella, which really only comes from chickens, so I never really got to eat it medium rare, which is how I would have liked it so I think I will just have some bread and water and leave. I wonder if they will validate my parking.

CHAPTER 10

"HOW DOES THE GIRL FIT INTO THE PICTURE?"

(POLICEMAN AT BEVERLY HILLS STATION, *SULLIVAN'S TRAVELS*)

"There's always a girl in the picture. What's the matter, don't you go to the movies?" —John L. Sullivan, *Sullivan's Travels*

Is becoming an entrepreneur a conscious decision or an inexorable event over which one has limited control? Can you decide to be one or are you simply sucked into its maw, trapped long before you find that the damn thing can bite you in painful places?

Starting in 2003 I spent five years teaching an MBA graduate course in entrepreneurship at San Diego State University, and on the first lecture of the first day of the first class I said the following:

"Ask for your money back if you think I can teach you to be an entrepreneur. I cannot teach you to be an entrepreneur. I can only teach some principles and some ways of thinking, but I am not a neuro-geneticist and cannot implant the appropriate DNA."

Over the past 15 years, I have come to even more fully believe that thesis. The stuff that empowers and forms the successful entrepreneur is not teachable. It comes from another space—deep in the dark recesses of the tortured soul.

Rule #19: Entrepreneurs do not do it for fame or fortune. They do it for revenge.

I believe that one of the primary drivers that ignites the entrepreneurial spirit is the simple desire for revenge, the fierce human desire to "get even."

My mother didn't love me.

My father thought I had a difficult personality.

My music teacher humiliated me in class.

That girl dumped me.

And so on and on and on.

The list is endless but certainly one of the primary human emotions is "I'll show that motherfucker that I am not the failure/ugly/stupid/weak/helpless/poor/defeated/inadequate person you think I am."

I believe that revenge is not only a powerful emotion, but also a positive one. Revenge comes from hurt places and it is the will to overcome the hurt that pushes people to excel beyond normal levels.

In my case, my father was most kind in giving me a boost toward entrepreneurship. When I was 17, he advised me that I had acquired a sufficiently difficult personality that I would never be able to work for or with anyone, so if I hoped to put food on my own table I would have to work for myself. Who else could tolerate me?

Note to file: Very helpful to self-image.

I was a pre-med student at Tufts University, and I came home at Christmas my sophomore year—with all "A's" in all my science classes: biology, chemistry, and physics—and I suggested to my dad that I would like to follow in his footsteps (he was a famous radiologist). I asked him if he thought it would be very cool for me to join him in his practice. Would he like to have a sign on his door, "Senturia and Son: Radiologists to the Stars"? He considered the idea for a moment, and then to make the point ever so succinctly, he simply said, "No."

And we both laughed. And when I went back to school I dropped out of pre-med and became an English major.

Rule #401: Revenge is not just a dish to be eaten cold or hot. Revenge is to be held close and nurtured and reviewed and studied and explored and embraced and then to be taken internally, whether orally or by syringe, into a dark, demon space and then used to create the fury of your own success.

If you think I am bit over the top here, please stand witness to the past 5,000 years of rage, war, and killing that we call modern civilization.

You get my point.

So for me, since I had been labeled incorrigible and unemployable by any organization with more than one other person working in it, I was pretty much forced to become my own boss, and so I have spent the ensuing 43 years trying to show my father (who died 20 years ago) that he was mistaken; that in fact I was not the failure that he had "magic markered" me with so long ago.

I am not unique in that way. Every person wages war against the long-ago demons and wrongs committed by various peoples against his or her person. And long after the physical forms have disappeared, the apparitions still remain.

But the good news is that the fierce drive for self-recognition informs a very large percentage of human excellence: the arts, the sciences, the humanities, the entire creation of our community of man and woman. We are all of us trying to exorcise that hurt, real or imagined, that happened so long ago.

Before I entered the real estate business, I had another profession, one that trains the entrepreneur in a rigorous way as to the various dealings and ways of the world in which the ever-changing alliances and human capital form a never-ending organic flow of money and creativity into which the yeast of courage and fear meld seamlessly into sex and power.

Rule #98: The only business more rotten than the used-car business is the movie business.

In 1971 I went to AFI and then on to Hollywood where I spent nine years in the movie business. I was a writer, and not particularly successful. I wrote a lot and a very little of my efforts got made. But I had an agent and I had lots of meetings. Hollywood is about taking meetings. The more you take, the better you feel even though your chances do not really improve. At the end of the day (and it is a long day of the locust) it is still who you know and who you blow.

A producer invited me to a breakfast meeting at the Beverly Wilshire hotel. I was being considered to do a rewrite of a famous Cary Grant movie called *Mr. Blandings Builds His Dream House.*

The Beverly Wilshire was very fancy: white tablecloths, snooty waiters. I was there to impress the gentleman with my deep grasp of screwball comedy. But being sensitive and impecunious (the eggs and bacon were $19), I ordered a grapefruit—just a simple grapefruit.

"No, I'm not hungry, more than enough, watching my figure yadda yadda." Big mistake. My first stab with the spoon directed a squirt into the producer's eye—just like in any Marx Brothers or Three Stooges movie.

He was not overly amused. I did get the job, but I got tossed after the first draft and someone else got the writing credit. To this day, I believe it was the grapefruit seed. Remember, "If your eye causes you to sin, pluck it out." —Mark 9:47

Grapefruits never bothered me personally. I wear glasses.

Rule #108: Never eat grapefruit at a breakfast meeting.

As for how people get jobs and how movies get made, it remains one of the great mysteries of the universe, on par with the number of quarks it takes to fill up a Hadron Collider.

Rule #232: "Nobody knows anything." —William Goldman, famous screenwriter, *Butch Cassidy and the Sundance Kid, All the President's Men,* among many others.

I loved the movie business. As rotten as it was, I loved it. And I found that it was marvelous training for my future careers in real estate and technology; if you can survive among the rats and cons and cheats and ego maniacs in Hollywood, then hell, deal making in real estate or technology or venture capital should be a no-brainer.

Rule #391: If a studio executive said no to every picture that was brought to him, he would have been right 82 percent of the time.

The reason I left Hollywood was simple: I wanted to be my own boss.

I remember vividly writing a 90-minute made-for-television script and taking it to a producer. He reads it, calls me into his office, says it made him laugh out loud, fall off his chair hilarious but listen kid, we are not buying comedies right now, we are buying dramas. So I said I would be back, and in seven weeks I came back to him with a tear-jerker, and he reads it and he calls me into his office and he says he used three handkerchiefs and he was so moved that he was gasping for air as he finished the last page but listen kid, right now the big boys, the boys at the top, they say no more dramas, they only want comedies—people need to laugh. That is when I reached across his desk and grabbed him by his tie and tried to strangle him. Shortly after, I left the movie business for good. Because it is no business at all. It may be 1,000 other things, but it is not a business.

Allow me to explain. In the movie business there is a concept called "net profits." Net profits are traditionally defined as gross receipts less all approved expenses. In theory, what's left is profit. This is a classic and generally accepted accounting principle.

In the movie business there is a famous definition in a studio contract of the words "net profits." This definition of net profits runs 63 pages, and to this day, no one in the history of cinema has ever seen any distribution from "net profits."

Winston Groom wrote the movie *Forrest Gump*, which did over $200 million in gross receipts. However, due to what is known as Hollywood accounting, Groom received nothing from his percentage of ownership in net profits.

One of the most famous cases of all is Art Buchwald, who sued Paramount. He had co-written the movie *Coming to America*, starring Eddie Murphy. It did $350 million in gross receipts, Buchwald got nothing, and he sued. The court found it "unconscionable" that there could be no net profits when the cost of the movie had been less than $30 million. Rather than disclose their actual accounting practices, the studio settled.

You call this a business?

So I went to night school at UCLA, studied real estate, and set about a new career. Along the way I jettisoned Hollywood and got rid of my first wife, who was an actress. Need I say more?

NEVER, EVER DISCOUNT THE POWER OF GOOD FORTUNE

(IT ALSO FAVORS *FORTUNE* MAGAZINE)

Rule #213: Never, ever discount the power of time and timing.

It was August 1995, and I was having lunch with Jim Nicholas in a small Vietnamese restaurant in Hillcrest, a few miles from downtown San Diego. We particularly liked the deep-fried spring rolls, and we used to go to this restaurant together about once every two weeks with the specific purpose of trying to figure out some stupid way we could lose money in some half-baked scheme.

Jim was a wealth of goofy ideas, and I loved him for them. We had been friends since 1986 although we had never done an actual deal together.

It was Tuesday, and the new edition of *Newsweek* had just come out. Inside was an article about the proliferation of Internet cafés. You could have a cup of coffee and surf the 'Net and maybe also get your e-mail. (Ironically, it was the Internet that contributed to *Newsweek* going out of business; the magazine was recently sold for a dollar and the assumption of $40 million in liabilities.)

Remember, this is 1995. E-mail was becoming significant but was still a little geeky and not yet pervasive. There was no Wi-Fi, no smart phones. Laptops were big and bulky. Going to a café for a latte and some e-mail seemed like a good idea.

Our chicken Penang arrived and was followed closely by Jim suggesting we open an Internet café to capitalize on the craze.

In 1990, I had invested in a restaurant called Fio's in the Gaslamp District of San Diego. It featured northern Italian, and was a smashing success. You could not get in without reservations, and they were available starting three weeks in advance. It was like one of those New York restaurants where you ask for a reservation and the maitre d' laughs and says, "What year?"

Rule #215: Time and timing.

It was December 28, 1990, and Fio's had opened 12 days earlier. The line was out the door, the crowd was gorgeous, they were drinking at the bar, and it was clearly a happening place.

I was sitting at a tiny table in the bar with my wife and a friend, and up walks the managing partner, Jack Berkman. Jack was a marvelous, larger than life, piece of work public relations guy. And he was really good at what he did. I had known him for a couple years and had even hired him on a deal. The guy could sling it with the best of them. He was hyped up, always on, could sell ice to Eskimos, and all I wanted to do was tell him how great his restaurant is and wish him well. Pausing to inhale only once, he blasts me for five minutes with how great this thing is going to be. I have a momentary lapse of Rational Man Behavior, and I say to him, "Can I get into the deal?"

If you put cocaine in front of an addict, you don't need to bring a straw.

Jack says, "It's your lucky day, I have two units left." We walk into the kitchen; I take one look around and tell him, "I'm in." I had no idea what I was looking at or what the deal was. I had seen no paperwork. I just needed a fix. A deal and some pasta. I'm there for you, baby: $25,000, two units, and bring some more Parmesan cheese.

Who really knew if they were the "last units" or whether Jack had gotten his Ph.D. at the Max Bialystock School of restaurant finance? All I knew was now I could get a table at the hottest restaurant in town.

Twelve years later, we sold the joint. By then I had gotten my money back almost twice (from a restaurant deal, I would call that amazing) and had used my 25 percent food discount enough to save another $10,000, so what's to complain about?

Rule #294: It is important to know the difference between blind, dumb luck and actually thinking you know what the fuck you are doing.

I was offered three more restaurant deals over the next five years. I turned down every one of them. Children should not play with sharp knives.

Being there on December 28 was just the right place at the right time. It did not confer on me any right to think I knew a duck breast from a chicken wing. Mario Batali is never going to take my call.

Which brings me back to telling Jim, "There is no fucking way that I am ever going back into the restaurant business, even if you call it an Internet café. However, what might be really cool is if you could get your e-mail in a public place, like an airport or a train station. Pass me the Tom Xao Girug."

Neither of us knew anything about the kiosk business but it did seem like a good idea, so I took a napkin and started to doodle.

At that time, Jim was the proud owner of an eight-unit apartment house directly across the street from the restaurant. It was called the Egyptian, and he had won a number of awards for its renovation and restoration. King Tut would have been most impressed.

So naturally, we drew the kiosk in the shape of a pyramid.

By the end of lunch, we had decided to go into the Internet kiosk business, providing public access to the Internet and e-mail.

Rule #193: There are always forces at play that you know nothing about. Try to understand them before it is too late.

It was August 1995 and three things were occurring simultaneously about which we either knew nothing or were only vaguely aware.

1.   The advent of the Pentium chip

2.   The rise and demand for 24/7 e-mail access
3.   Windows 95

The idea of an Internet kiosk had been kicked around long before us but it was only until #1 and #3 came to pass that the cost of being able to do it was close to semi-reasonable. In other words, this was an idea that could only be brought to feasible fruition when a combination of certain technical hurdles were overcome.

The hurdles were jumped in September 1995, which is exactly when we started.

Prior to that time, with DOS and slower chips, the cost to produce a kiosk with even slow speed functionality would have been around $50,000. Using Windows and Pentium, the cost dropped to $15,000, and it would work pretty damn well.

We had a chance.

So with our entire market research effort being that copy of *Newsweek* and believing our own bullshit, we were off and running.

Next up there was the small matter of technology. Neither one of us could program a VCR. We went looking for a genius.

Rule #129: When marrying, if you have a choice, pick brains over money.

I had met Ms. Barbara Bry in October 1993. How we met is another rule for another time, but by 1995, we were dating and in love. She knew everyone in technology in San Diego because of her position as the director of programs at UC San Diego CONNECT. CONNECT was an "incubator without walls," which had as its mission the goal of connecting entrepreneurs with the resources they needed to become successful. My bride-to-be also happened to be a Harvard MBA.

Rule #246: When the woman in your life is smarter than you are, don't get confused by the male gene for pride and stupidity. First, ask. And if that doesn't work, then beg.

"BB ["Darling" would be an appropriate word to use at this time also], can you help me find and hire a genius for this brilliant [half-baked] idea?"

Let's be honest, the real estate business was in the tank. I was almost done with my divorce and I needed a new career. I had no credentials in technology or software but you know that you should never let the truth get in the way of a good story, so, in the classic entrepreneurial model—since no one would hire me—I decided to hire myself.

And she knew just who to call: Mark Fackler, CEO of Stellcom.

Stellcom was an engineering development and services firm. They were in the business of solving problems and building things. You brought them a technology problem, and they had 30+ engineers/developers/geniuses on staff. They would bid the job based on hours and complexity, and lo and behold and presto, out the other end would come your product.

So I went to see Mr. Fackler. I told him the idea, and said I wanted to hire his firm. He listened and then said, "No thank you. Not interested in the deal."

(Here we go again. When people talk about been there, done that, I think this is what they are really referring to.)

"No, you don't understand. I need you to build this for me. This is a really good idea." I was headed toward begging.

"No, you don't understand. I am not interested."

"But I need someone to build this for me."

"Great. Go find someone else."

Rule #231: "No" is just a speed bump on the road to "Yes," even if it is said emphatically and in capital letters.

I waited a few days and called Mark back. He agreed to see me a second time. I was impassioned and explained with hand gestures and a PowerPoint how I would pay him, give him stock in the new company, and that this adventure would put his firm on the map. Once again, let's just touch the reality stone for a moment. He was already successful and on the map. It was me who was a nobody.

Still he was firm in his decision and again clearly indicated that this was not a job he wanted. He was busy; he didn't want to be bothered. And frankly, he also said he wasn't sure that it could actually be done.

I was now batting zero for two, and I could see that a continued frontal assault was not going to be effective. OK, Fackler, grab your ankles. There is more than one way to cross the moat and storm the Bastille.

Rule #131: Your most important asset is human capital. Listen closely when they are lamenting. It is then that you will learn what it takes to make them happy and keep them toiling at sharpening the swords. Failure to listen closely can lead to a revolution and the unintended use of said swords.

The president of Stellcom was a fellow named Peter Van Horne. And believe me, he actually was a genius. Fackler did the business deals, and Van Horne built the rocket ships that would go to the moon.

So I contacted Mr. Van Horne and invited him for a cup of coffee.

Rule #89: The lament is never solely about money.

It turns out that Peter loved technology and was intrigued by the idea. He was intellectually engaged and wondered if it even could be done. (It was fall of 1995 and Windows and Pentium were still brand new to the development community.)

After an hour, the conversation turned to my agenda, and the real substance of the meeting. Peter was unhappy at Stellcom. He had been chafing under Mr. Fackler. I probed further and found that underneath this mild-mannered, buttoned-up tech genius lurked an entrepreneur yearning to be free. He wanted to drive his own boat. (Peter was an accomplished sailor.)

And it seemed to me that Peter could be pried loose. The plan was simple. If I could spin a tale of sixpence, a pocketful of rye, and the dream of untold riches, then I could lure him away from his terrific, secure job, currently paying him $225,000 per year, to become the Chief Technology Officer of my start-up at $85,000 per year, plus a significant chunk of stock and freedom to be his own boss (sort of, after all, I was still the CEO, but that was a mere minor technicality in my mind).

Truth is, after I began to probe, it became clear to me that Peter was definitely the kind of guy you could build a company on. I could definitely ride this horse into the sunset. Billy Crystal and the Duke were going to team up and brand us some Internet cattle.

Peter had a big ego. But he had an even bigger brain.

Rule #56: Be willing to make trade-offs.

Everyone has studied Greek mythology; we all know about the Trojan horse. Get your spurs and saddle up. You don't want to end up all hat and no cattle.

So I went back to Mr. Fackler and made the following deal.

"Mark, I perfectly understand that this project does not fit into the classic Stellcom model, and I respect that, and I am appreciative that you have let me chat with Peter about it. It seems that Peter has some mild technical curiosity in this, and so I propose that you let Peter noodle on it for a few hours in the evenings and on the weekends, on his own time of course, and I will just pay Stellcom $5,000 as a consulting fee."

Simple. Fackler gets some money without having to lose any billable time, and I get a chance to infiltrate Peter's brain and implant a deep desire to grab this brass ring and ride into his own sunset.

Fackler considered my proposal.

"Two weeks. All you get is two weeks. I need him back full-time, focused on what I am doing here."

"You have a deal."

I now had the green light to work on Van Horne while he worked on the project.

Rule #121: How ya gonna keep 'em down on the farm after they've seen Paree?

Within a month, Van Horne had left Stellcom and become the CTO of my fledgling company, Atcom.

Rule # 6: The heart often yearns for things that money cannot buy.

CHAPTER 12

GEORGE W. BUSH GREW UP IN TEXAS. SO DID GARY AVERY

(ONE OF THEM WOULD HAVE MADE A GOOD PRESIDENT)

Rule # 345: At the beginning of every adventure, one or two people will prove to be invaluable. They are seldom the people you think they will be.

It was the fall of 1995, and Peter had begun to build the software. I was racing around raising money from friends, family, and fools.

And I got the idea that we should do some promotion. Time to tell the world what was coming, even if we had no fucking idea if we could even build it, let alone when it would be coming—if at all.

But you remember truth and a good story. So, once more into the breach.

Rule #491: A picture is worth a thousand words. Fred Barnard first said this in an advertising trade journal called *Printers Ink*. The date: 1921.

So I hired a graphic artist to draw a picture of this pyramid kiosk. After all, if someone were going to buy this radical new brilliant device, they might want to know what it looked like.

So I hired the best guy I knew in San Diego: Don Hollis. His job was to draw a picture of what didn't exist and make it look fabulous, out of this world. Which he did. A multi-colored kiosk, floating in a star-lit black heavenly sky, promising out-of-this-world access to the universe. It looked as if George Lucas had conspired with Tutankhamen. A pyramid-shaped rocket ship launched into the future of Internet communication. We could never afford to build what he drew, but remember:

Rule #109: Never let the truth stand in the way of a good story.

So we pressed on.

And then we got a break. We gave the picture to Jackie Townsend, who was the CEO of her own public relations firm. She had a great reputation in San Diego and was very successful at blowing your horn. She could get coverage for your fledgling string quartet as if you were the Boston Symphony Orchestra.

We hired her and the firm, and we made my favorite kind of deal. We paid a fair but modest fee for her work and then set up a bonus program that included more cash and stock if she were successful. Success was defined as getting us mentioned or noticed in any one of seven different publications. For example, no points for the local paper. Jackpot for *The Wall Street Journal* with assorted in-between bonus levels.

Rule #322: Make sure everyone on the boat has a chance to sit on the top deck in the sun.

So Jackie, armed with the outrageous picture of the flying kiosk in the sky, set out to make Atcom famous before its time.

And she did just that.

The second week of January 1996, on the back page of *Business Week*, at the very bottom of the page on the left side, was a very short article about an e-mail kiosk coming to an airport near you, with the color picture of our flying kiosk.

We had hit the big time.

Rule #1: Return every e-mail and every phone call.

We were rolling along now with software development. But we had the usual and classic problem of finding a customer who would let us put this damn thing in their location.

Our business model was simple. We paid to build it, we put it in a public place, and we shared the revenue derived from users swiping their credit cards and checking their e-mails and surfing the Web.

That business model ranked somewhere between flawed and stupid. We did not know this at the time but we were headed toward going broke. You don't know what you don't know, especially at the time you don't know it.

One thing we learned rather quickly is that public places have lots of vendors who want to put stuff in them (precisely because they are public places with lots of people), and they have so many vendors wanting to be there that they get to charge rent—a fixed fee—whether anybody uses it or not. Shared revenue is the kicker on top of base rent. Nice.

I argued vigorously that we were not like a hot dog stand or a sunglass store. We were providing a needed service in the furtherance of American commerce and personal productivity.

Apparently a lot of other people before me had tried this argument. Paying rent was the accepted model if you wanted to put your crap in a public place. Everyone pays. What the hell makes your Internet kiosk so special, dude?

And then the phone rang. I was out at a meeting. Nicole Rockstead, my executive assistant, who has been with me since 1993, took the call. The message she relayed to me was that someone from Texas had phoned. She said he was a bit abrupt, and she could not fully understand what he wanted given his accent, but I should call him back.

A man with a big Texas accent comes booming through on his speakerphone and says he works with General Telephone and Electronics. At the time, GTE was the largest of the independent U.S. telephone companies.

"I saw a picture of that kiosk thing in *Business Week*. I would like to get some of them for the Dallas-Fort Worth airport, where we are the exclusive provider of phone and Internet," says Gary Avery, VP of worldwide everything for GTE.

Rule #256: The customer is always right. Even if he wants pastrami on white bread with mayo, give it to him.

"How many do you think you will need?"

"Twenty should be about right."

"When would you like them?"

"Spring. No later than April 1."

"No problem. You'll have them installed, ready to go, no later than April 1."

And that was the end of the phone call. I was so amazed, that I called back a day later just to see if there really was a Gary Avery who worked at GTE. Maybe it was a prank or a delusion that I needed to discuss with my shrink. The receptionist who answered the phone confirmed that Mr. Avery was indeed a big shot and was in a meeting.

"Well, don't interrupt him. I'll call back later."

By the way, we had not yet built even one of the kiosks, and the software didn't work either.

Rule #202: The reason to sell something that doesn't exist is that deadlines can be liberating.

I explained to the team that we now had a customer who wanted to pay for something that we were making. We had a due date, which was something to push back against—or drown trying.

And to the credit of the entire team, the kiosks got designed, built, and installed in the Dallas-Fort Worth airport by the middle of April.

I look back on that little article in *Business Week*, it was less than 15 lines, and I remain in complete awe and wonder that it launched the company.

Rule #48: One big customer can also bury a company.

Reams have been written about rule #48, and I will not repeat the obvious.

The lure of the big customer is like cocaine. With the first snort, you think all your problems are solved. You want to go on an elephant hunt. But when you come down off the high and desperately want to do it again, you find that there are only so many elephants. After a while, you have to hunt ducks.

Rule #71: Publicity is powerful, especially if your name is spelled correctly.

We were rolling along now and could quickly see that we were going to need more money. We had raised $1 million from friends, family, and fools and another $1 million from some of the more unusual suspects—including some money from an optometrist I met on a ski lift in Park City, Utah.

Rule #2: Networking is a profession. Become a professional at it. And that means having an elevator pitch that can be delivered in less than the six minutes it takes for the ski lift to get to the top of the mountain.

But we could not get professional venture capital financing. And their reason, while infuriating to me, was perfectly rational and obvious to them. They were not going to invest in a technology company with an untested, untried, novice CEO. My previous career counted for nothing to the venture capitalists. Without the secret handshake, I was never going to get into the fraternity. Skull and Bones, my ass!

I will forgo a detailed rant on the venture capital community— viewed by me as troglodytes defined as creatures of primitive character, who emerged from the mists of time, untouched by human evolution. I think you get my drift.

The begging made me absolutely nuts. We would go up to Silicon Valley, meet with some junior nobody in the firm who would show some interest in the idea and the company, and then ask the question:

"Well, who is going to be the CEO?"

And of course this junior dickhead would say this directly to me, the current and as far as I could tell, more than adequate CEO. But I'm a practicing student of Rational Man Behavior. "Write me a check, and you can put Bozo the Clown in as CEO if you want."

Once you indicated that you were willing to be fired upon funding, then you might get to meet the senior dickhead. And it was then that you found out that they were never going to fund even if Jack Welch was the CEO. They just wanted to horse you around a bit, pick your brain, get some competitive information, and then put you back on Southwest Airlines with the vague tangential carrot dangling fishhook, "Let us think about it some more, and we'll get back to you." But of course, they never did. These guys must have studied at the Hollywood Producers School of Never Say "No." The rule in the movie business is you never give a definitive "no" because you do not want to be the schmuck who turns down Spielberg's movie about a shark. Always better to say, "Interesting, we'll get back to you." Don't you just love that kind of courage, leadership, spine, and conviction?

This problem of getting a chance to do something before you have proven that you can do it is one that haunts everyone. It is the syndrome of the first job. The venture capital world reminded me that I had once again fallen into the *Alice in Wonderland* hell hole of Hollywood. I wanted to reach across the desk, grab the guy by the tie (even though VCs don't wear ties), and strangle the motherfucker, just like I did to that film producer 20 years ago.

You can't get an agent until you have sold something, and you can't sell something without an agent. You can't get in the union until you have a job, and you can't get a job if you are not in the union.

Rule #75: You can't—until you can.

In retrospect, maybe the model actually works because somehow lots of people figure it out. Survival of the fittest. It is the Rubik's Cube of the secret handshake. Remind me, please, which finger I insert where.

For the next year, the continual reminder of my total inadequacy (at least in their minds) stoked my anger and fueled my laser focus.

Rule #19: Entrepreneurs do not do it for fame or fortune. They do it for revenge. Go see the Facebook movie.

I am quite honest about my motivations. I have been seeking revenge for all the slights, real or imagined, I have received since my mother and father suggested that I would never amount to much. There is nothing original about this feeling. It's the "I will show them!" syndrome that, properly harnessed, has fueled innovation for countless centuries. From these passions (although psychiatrically misplaced, Freud might say, but did he discover the cure for cancer?), great achievements in technology, finance, manufacturing, medicine, etc., have been created. A little guilt can go a long way. Innovation is fueled by the misery of the human condition.

Were it not for the fact that all parents screw up their kids in some way, man would never have evolved past the Stone Age. After all, I am sure that there were some gorillas back then who abused their children, which led them to get back at their parents and discover fire.

Evolution. Stanley Kubrick has the greatest jump-cut in the history of cinema, in the movie *2001* when the apes throw the bone up in the air and it comes down as the spaceship Discovery.

It was the spring of 1997, and we had gotten a few customers. There were a lot of articles about us. After all, public access to the Internet was now becoming more pervasive. But we had a burn rate problem. "Burn rate" is a simple concept. It is what it costs to stay in business each month. And we were losing $130,000 per month. Inelegantly speaking, if we did not raise more money we were headed to the famous last line of every movie: *The End.*

Rule #216: Objects in the mirror are closer than they appear.

But we were in trouble. Our family-friends-fools crowd was tapped out. The VC community was uninterested. But we were unable to dramatically cut our burn rate because we now had customers. We had done the Dallas airport, and now were set to do La Guardia as well as two convention centers, and we were talking to the Atlanta airport.

Every airport wanted the gizmo, so we had developers and salespeople and marketing and installation. We had 27 people who wanted to get paid every two weeks (some nerve!).

And we came to April 1997. We had enough money for one more payroll, and then we were done.

You remember Jeremy Cohen, my partner from the Hilton/ Cobb/Architectonica/Gaslamp fiasco. By this time, Cohen and his boss, Malkin, were rolling along with their hotel project. All had been forgiven. They had approvals, and the future looked bright. In a moment of madness, Jeremy had personally invested $25,000 in Atcom, so I had a fierce desire not to let him down. Over our weekly coffee meeting, I relayed my plight to him, and he said he might know one fellow: a real estate investor by the name of Allan Simon.

Rule #23: Keeping your problems to yourself ensures that no one else can help you. If you don't give out your address, how can anybody find your house?

Simon was a piece of work: rich, charming, handsome, smart. He was a big guy with white hair and a marvelous smile. And best of all, he had a very decisive nature. In his own words, "I am a fast gun."

We met several times. He asked a lot of questions. Nine days later, he invested $800,000 and went on the Board. We had dodged another bullet.

CHAPTER 13

FORTUNE FAVORS THE BOLD

(IT ALSO FAVORS *FORTUNE* MAGAZINE)

Rule #55: One good deed deserves another. So, what have you done for me lately?

Having launched the company with GTE, Ms. Jackie Townsend re-enters the fray, yet again. Always bet on the jockey.

At that time *Fortune* magazine had a feature called "The 25 Coolest Companies in America." They published the list once a year, and getting on it was a big deal. Previous winners included Netscape, Cisco, and US Robotics.

Each year, *Fortune* looked around the country and tried to pick the top 25, which were often companies with a lot of "buzz." And for sure, if Atcom had nothing else, it had buzz. By then, Jackie had gotten our little company mentioned 178 times in various publications. Not much revenue but lots of buzz.

Clearly, we needed scale. We had about 55 kiosks in various places, and to get to break-even, we would need 500. And to scale, we needed money, so we could get customers, so we could get big enough to sell to someone dumber but bigger than we were, who would gladly overpay to acquire the team and the technology. Welcome to Milo Minderbinder meets Start-Up 22. (*Catch-22* is one of my favorite books.)

So we asked Jackie to work her magic to get us into *Fortune* magazine.

Rule #230: If it were easy, anybody could do it.

There was no secret handshake and no magic formula but she did get us an interview. A young woman from the magazine called from New York and interviewed me for an hour.

Long ago, while I was at AFI, I served as an intern on the Billy Wilder movie *Front Page*. And when Billy wanted greatness in a scene, instead of merely saying "Action," he would often tell his actors, "Give me both knees."

Believe me, I gave this young writer every body part I had in an effort to charm her into believing that we belonged in the pantheon of the 25. In addition to the interview, we had to send reams of material justifying our claim to greatness.

In the end it came down to the last two spots—us and one other company. They would not tell us which one they were going to pick but they did come out to take a picture, just in case. I knew that the picture was going to be the determinant. It had to grab you. None of this two people hunched over a computer with a scrawled whiteboard in the background.

This was San Diego. Beach, bikinis, surf, and sand.

Rule #227: Whenever possible, play to your strength.

We put one of the kiosks (108 pounds) onto a truck and by laying track and using a dolly, we were able to move it out onto the sand next to the Ocean Beach pier, waves lapping at the base. Then I stood on the keyboard tray (thus demonstrating its tensile strength and indestructibility) with Peter Van Horne sitting at the base. And when the sun set into the horizon, complete with green flash, the *Fortune* photographer shot the photo.

I am there for you, baby!

Image matters. Form over substance. True cool.

And five weeks later, we were in *Fortune* magazine as one of the 25 coolest companies in America. More stock for Ms. Townsend!

And then we got another out-of-the-blue phone call.

"Hello, my name is Tom Caldwell. I work at Microsoft and I would like to come down and meet you."

Rule #91: This is what is known as good news and bad news. The good news: Microsoft is calling. The bad news: Microsoft is calling. And thus began our "partnership" with Bill and the boys from Redmond. It turned out they didn't want to crush us; they wanted to help us (to help them).

Rule #317: Do not ever underestimate the power of good weather.

Caldwell came, he saw, he conquered, he stayed. We lured him away from Mr. Gates with sunshine and stock options. Tom became our head of engineering. He simply could not face going back to Seattle for another winter of cold and rain.

As we were about to finalize our deal with Tom, I asked him a question.

"Just curious, how did Bill Gates decide to send you down to see us?"

And Tom told the following story:

"I was called into a meeting with Bill, and on the table was the *Fortune* magazine article and around the table were a dozen of his lieutenants, and he simply went around the room and told each of us to go and research one of these companies. He had already picked the ones he thought would be of interest to Microsoft, and he simply told us to get on a plane, learn everything we could, and report."

"Of all the gin joints in all the towns in all the world, she walks into mine." —Rick Blaine, *Casablanca*

So now we had more buzz and more muscle and more money but we had still not figured out how to make a real company—the kind with a sustainable business model that generates that elusive Loch Ness monster called positive cash flow.

Rule #228: The best ideas often come from the factory floor. Make sure the floor has a direct elevator to management.

We had sent a team to do the installation at La Guardia, and it was a tough one. (What did you expect, Neil? This is New York City, and even though your last name ends in a vowel, that does not mean you are a member of the five families.)

And on the flight home one of our young employees, David Pattison, comes up with a simple, yet brilliant idea.

Rule #93: Do not hide the truth from your people. If they do not know the boat is sinking, they will not be looking for a life raft until it's too late. On the other hand, if they are aware that the water is rising around their feet, they will be highly focused on trying to plug the leak.

It was clear to everyone on the team that the kiosk business was not going to work. It was a "take-rate" problem. Not enough people were willing to pay to access the Internet.

The software (to Peter's credit) was amazing and worked really well but it turned out that people did not really like to access their e-mail in public places, in part due to privacy issues and in part because they did not want to pay. In the trials, when it was free, we had daily usage above five hours per kiosk. When we asked them to swipe a credit card and pay the piper, we got an average of 49 minutes per kiosk. Our take-rate was going to take us right out of business.

David comes into my office the next morning and says simply, "The software is pretty cool [David was 24] so why not use it in hotels? I was at the Holiday Inn for three nights, and the dial-up for my laptop was miserable. Slow, dropped me constantly, could not get any work done. Painful slow. We could simply put our software on a high-speed router, wire up the hotel rooms. It's almost a no-brainer."

Actually, it was a brainer. A really big brainer.

I may have neglected to mention that the Atcom solution was for high-speed Internet connectivity. Big pipe, high speed. The AOL dial-up era was still with us but for the power user, business traveler, dial-up was a disaster. Files, access, security, VPN—the list of aggravations was long.

Rule #94: Listen carefully. Good ideas may be spoken softly.

David was not a technical evangelist or an MBA. He was a simple surfer dude who just wandered upstairs to share an interesting thought. Nice thought. It would save the company and make us all rich.

And thus began Atcom 2.0, the reinvention—the wiring of high-speed connectivity in hotel rooms for business travelers who had laptops, needed privacy, access to corporate files, and wanted high-speed bandwidth and security. And would pay for it.

But as far as the venture capital world knew, we were still up to our necks in the kiosk business. Our strategy change was only in the process of being implemented.

It turned out that the *Fortune* magazine article not only grabbed the attention of Mr. Gates, it also prompted a call from a venture capitalist.

I get a call from Mr. Tom Hirschfeld, a senior associate at a large and famous venture capital company in New York, Patricof Ventures, whose namesake, Alan Patricof, is sometimes considered the father of venture capital investing.

"My name is Tom Hirschfeld, and my boss, Alan Patricof, has a son living in Atlanta, and he is considering getting into the Internet kiosk business. Would you mind if we chatted [a.k.a. picked my brains] a bit about the opportunity [which we have no intention of funding]?"

A venture capitalist was calling us. Must have been a wrong number. That had never happened before. It had always been us calling them, us begging them, us failing to get past the junior nobody, us heading out the door. So what if Tom's call had nothing to do with funding our current business, that it was intelligence gathering for the son of his boss and that nothing was likely to come of it for Atcom. No good deed goes unpunished. And you can never be faulted for telling the truth.

So I had a long call with Mr. Hirschfeld. I told him what a lousy business idea the kiosk game was and that Alan should tell his son to give up this insane get-rich-quick scheme because it would only lead to rebuke, dismay, unrequited love, and significant capital losses that his father could use on his tax return.

Rule #81: Find the subtext. Things are never quite what they seem to be.

It turns out that what Alan really wanted was two things. One, to get his arms around how the kiosk business really worked; after all, we were the leaders in the business, such as it was. Two, for me to convince his son to not go into that business.

Alan wanted his son to finish college and then go to business school. The son, on the other hand, dazzled by the possibility of Internet riches in 1997 and desiring to get out from under the old man's thumb, wanted to take his inheritance early and set out to blaze his own trail. He was smitten by the entrepreneurial bug. But his father wanted to use me as a can of Raid.

In Alan's mind, his son's entrepreneur thing was a just a distraction toward the goal of getting a real education and ultimately a decent job as a hard-working, contributing member of society—especially if it was New York Society.

You gotta love America. One of the most famous venture capitalists in the world wanted me, a fierce entrepreneur, to convince his son to not go into the business and not to follow his own star but instead be a good son and go back to school.

And if I were successful in convincing the son that the kiosk business sucked, how was I going to then convince his dad that in fact our new idea was going to be the best business in the world, and that our company was worthy of venture investment?

It turned out that Tom Hirschfeld had studied the classics as well as American and British literature. I had been an English major at Tufts University so our initial interaction was 90 minutes of literary allusions, followed by the repartee of obscure quotes from long-dead authors in an effort to demonstrate to each other that we were highly educated with useless information, suitable only for a *College Bowl* toss-up question concerning *The Dead Poets' Society*. Bottom line: Tom was a charm.

Little did I know that Shakespeare and Chaucer would be the glue that finally sealed our deal. But believe me, it was extremely slow-drying glue.

First, I talked the son out of doing kiosks and suggested that he listen to his father and finish school. Second, I pointed out to

Mr. Hirschfeld that our new business model, wiring hotel rooms, was brilliant. And third, as usual and as always, we were running out of money. Perhaps Alan would like to invest in our company and turn hotel rooms into gold.

Tom asked, "Where do you want this killin' done?"

"Out on Highway 61."

And so I flew to New York to meet with Mr. Hirschfeld and Mr. Alan Patricof.

Rule #408: Knowing the difference between RAM and ROM is nice but a working knowledge of Shakespeare and Dylan can carry you a long way.

Big office, fancy digs, very impressive conference room. They said, "No."

Back to San Diego. But I kept pestering Tom, calling him often to tell him of our "wins" in the hotel space.

Back to New York a second time. Met with Gene Levy, another senior big shot. Close but no cigar. But I was becoming a fixture; the receptionist knew my name. I was the guy who came every three months to get his brains beat in. Would you like a cup of coffee (in a real china teacup, no paper here)?

More telephone discussion. We were trying to be there for him, baby.

Back to New York a third time to meet Alan and all the partners. The really big conference room. Four new characters, plus the original Broadway cast, to work us over.

He shoots. He scores. In the corner of the end zone, both feet inbound. Nothing but net. Five million. Thank you very much.

Walking to the door, out came the triple fishhook. "Of course, we will need to get a world-class CEO to run the company."

"Sure, naturally, whatever, world class, no problem, sign me up. Maybe Jobs or Ellison. You name it. Not just a good one, not just a great one, but goddamnit, world class, nothing less. You betcha."

Rule #240: I never forget. And that crap about revenge is a dish best served cold? Bullshit! Revenge tastes good at any temperature.

And thus began the Patricof/Microsoft/Atcom adventure to wire the hotels of the world.

Like any Dennis Lehane book, there were another 39 twists still to come during the next 15 months. The company entered February 1999 running out of money again. So what else is new?

And oh, yes, we got a world-class CEO that spring.

Rule #221: If you can't find something nice to say about someone, don't say anything at all. —Ancient Proverb

Rule #282: Rule #221 is utter and complete bullshit. If the guy is a fucking dummy, tell him that to his face.

Let it suffice that our new CEO was a gentleman I despised. After about three years of significant effort and indeed some reasonable success, I was asked to politely turn over the reins to a short, intellectually challenged, sycophant anointed by Hirschfeld and Patricof, who would take over and take charge. At a salary that was nearly double what I was being paid but after all, he was world class. What do you expect? The Board had done an executive search, Jack Welch was not available, and the next 183 choices turned us down. You get what you get.

Rule #77: No one likes to be replaced. Repeat after me: No one likes to be replaced. All together now: No one likes to be replaced. This explains why wives get annoyed when you replace them with someone else. That is also why ex-wives want to rip your heart out, take you to the cleaners, and remove certain of your body parts. The same is true of ex-husbands. Tit for tat, so to speak. I'm not sure where the tat is located, but I am sure it is available to be ripped out.

With respect to the new CEO, like Lord Voldemort, I cannot speak his name.

And so we come to June 1999. I have been kicked upstairs to Chairman of the Board, which is code for "Stay out of the building, shut up, and bring me some coffee."

Rule #57: There is always a competitor. Followers of Sun Tzu understand this axiom well. Make your competitor your ally.

In the high-speed Internet in the hotel room racket, there were two real companies, and one of them was us. We had great, truly world-class software but we had nowhere near enough money. The other company? CAIS Internet. CAIS had gone public during the insanity of May 1999 and had raised $100 million. Their software sucked but they had a shitload of cash.

And they had a very interesting CEO: Ulysses Auger II.

From time to time over the previous couple of years, Ulysses and I had chatted on the phone. We ran into each other at conventions, and generally there was no love lost between us. He was bidding on hotels. We were bidding on hotels. He was a competitor.

The difference was that he had $100 million in the bank and we were dying a dog's death. We had gone out in the spring of 1999 to raise a round of financing, and even with our new world-class CEO who shall not be named, we came up empty.

In the spring of 1999, the hotel industry had decided that high-speed Internet in the rooms was not only a good idea, but in fact, a must-have. And in late May, four large hotel chains put up for bid almost 200,000 rooms. They had a simple proposition. Find a company willing to pay to install the system and then share the revenue from usage. The cost to install, all in, was about $300 per room so the ticket to swallow the whole banana was about $60 million. This was the moment. This was the Holy Grail. The guy who won the hotel room contracts was going to be the big winner.

It was a lot of dough, but with a good Excel spreadsheet, some wild-ass assumptions about the take-rate, a wing, a prayer, and an "exuberant" stock market, you could almost prove that this was a terrific opportunity.

And CAIS and Atcom were bidding against each other. Admittedly, we did not have the $60 million but I assumed that if we could win the contract, we could raise it. It was a little bit of "Sir, I assure you financing will not be a problem. We have a bunch of investors ready to go, as soon as you pick us."

But the hotel boys were no dopes. Hyatt, Hilton, Radisson, Four Seasons, Embassy Suites kept asking us to "sharpen our pencils." The more we both sharpened, the smaller the pencils got. We were down to a golf-cart-size stub.

Remember Rule #3, the one about going to events and meetings that you know will be a total waste of time?

In June 1999, there was a big Internet hospitality technology conference with 1,500 of our closest friends. Vendors were peddling everything digital for the hotel industry. Every company had a booth, trying to convince anyone within shouting distance that RevPar would go up dramatically if only the hotelier installed, bought, or used the Next Big Thing.

The world was abuzz with technology and deals. Twenty-one-year-olds were flipping companies from a napkin for $400 million.

You remember Rule #3. It is the Mother of All Rules. So off to the conference.

Atcom had a very small space in the giant, free-standing Microsoft booth. We had made it into the big tent but we were located right behind where the elephants do their thing.

If you have ever been to one of these kinds of conventions, you will recognize the ubiquitous Booth Babe. This is a beautiful young woman who greets prospective customers with a smile and cleavage and then directs the smitten prospect to a marketing/sales/customer service/I'm there for you, baby closer.

The booth babes at CAIS were out of this world.

Each of the hotel companies came by our booth to discuss the deal. Do the demo, allay concerns, and promise the digital future. We explained how the $60 million was no problem. If we got the contract, we could raise it.

CAIS, on the other hand, had a slightly better argument. The money was in the bank. Plus the booth babes. Not quite a fair fight.

It was a grueling event. Atcom did win a big hospitality Microsoft developer trophy. It was prestigious and certainly validated our software but let's be honest, it did not come with a check. We would be broke in 90 days, so I figured I would just add the award to the other crap when the vultures picked over our bones during the eventual asset sale. My Rosebud.

Still trying to raise money, we came back to San Diego. This game of musical chairs was going to end with a trombone up our ass.

I had chased all over the country for dough, including hiring an investment banker (Volpe, Brown, Whelan) to assist us. This included a trip to Alaska in early June to fly fish for salmon because big shots and venture capitalists would be there. Nineteen fishermen. Not one fish caught in five days. It was too early in the season. That explains why the promoters got a great rate. It also tells you something about investment banking.

And the hotel contracts were going to be let by the middle of August. And then I got a simple idea.

Rule #263: "Collusion" is just another word for "joint venture."

It was the Tuesday morning right after the Fourth of July, and we had enough money to make payroll and pay our expenses through September 16. I called Ulysses Auger II on the telephone, and herewith is a summary of our telephonic interaction (after the usual pleasantries).

"Look, Ulysses, you know that we are not the best of friends but there is no good reason for both of us to keep fighting for these contracts. There really isn't room for both of us. One company should remain standing, and the other one should go away. In essence, Ulysses, this town isn't big enough for the two of us." (This mantra came trippingly off my tongue since I had assiduously studied at the John Wayne/Gary Cooper school for the advancement of the Western film genre.)

When Ulysses did not hang up on me, I took my cue to continue.

"We have the best software. You know it, and the hotel companies know it. I have spoken to the Hilton people and they love our software. So I discussed it with my Board of Directors, and we have decided we should present a unified front and consolidate our offering. Bottom line, we would like to buy your company."

"Huh."

There is a silence. You know the rule about the guy who talks first loses. So, don't speak.

There is some sputtering on the other end of the line.

Ulysses was a proud man. After all, his parents gave him the name of one of the most famous Greeks, the King of Ithaca, the hero of Homer's poem, *The Odyssey*. This was not a man to be trifled with.

On the other hand, Faulkner had a few things to say about second generations in Yoknapatawpha County. Being an English major, I was betting on Wee Willie.

After a long pause, Mr. Auger spoke calmly but forcefully.

"Look, you little shit, I don't care for you either. But if anybody is going to be doing any buying, it is going to be us buying you out. You got that?"

I delivered a studied silence. Then . . .

"If that's how you feel, OK. You can buy us."

And six weeks hence (with about $40,000 left in our bank account) CAIS bought Atcom for $55 million that later—with earn-outs and kickers—turned into $75 million. If he had waited, he probably could have bought our whole company for a bag of banjo picks. We would have been dead meat.

Rule #314: It doesn't matter what you pay for something when you buy it. It only matters what you sell it for later.

Our deal closed on 9-9-99. Total invested capital in Atcom was $7.6 million, so everyone did nicely. The world-class CEO kept his job and ultimately went to work at Cisco. The employees and consultants who took some of their compensation in stock instead of cash did very well.

Seven months later, CAIS turned around and sold our software to Cisco Systems for $140 million. Those boys in Yoknapatawpha County are not as dumb as they look.

But I know the truth. We were lucky.

I had played a little Kahneman on him. I knew that he would feel insulted and outraged at my arrogance and audacity. Some nerve. Here I was without a pot to pee in, and I was threatening to buy him out.

His response was predictable: *I'll show you!*

And of course, he did.

But he could just as easily have hung up the phone and let me twist slowly, slowly in the wind.

Two years later, CAIS went bankrupt, and the stock price had dropped to less than a dollar.

And the end of the story is the one that fascinates me the most. I actually spoke with Ulysses one last time in late 2001. We were both at some event in D.C. I went up to him and commiserated. I felt badly for him. I do not dance on anyone's grave. That obloquy belongs to Sam Zell. I felt true empathy for Ulysses. He clearly was a beaten man.

Quietly, he put his arm on my shoulder and said the following:

"At the height of the boom, I was worth over $300 million in CAIS stock—but I never sold one share."

CHAPTER 14

CERTAIN FLOWERS TAKE LONGER TO BLOOM THAN OTHERS

The century plant, *agave Americana*, takes on average 25 years to bloom. It only blossoms once in its life, with the flowering spike growing so large (up to 35 feet) and so fast that it saps all the plant's resources, and then it dies. The plant is called the century plant because it blooms "once in a century."

My sense of the world at this point is that we have become obsessed with speed and with time. One way in which this is expressed: "I need to make my first million by the age of 30 or I am a failure."

And the Internet has exponentially exacerbated this neurotic, arbitrary, irrational measurement.

I was labeled with the "late bloomer syndrome" early in my life. It was my parents' way of dealing with the fact that I was not measuring up to their expectations, so rather than tell me that I was a failure, they simply advised me that I was a late bloomer.

Rule #411: Try to enjoy the journey because when you get there, the only thing left to do is check out.

CHAPTER 15

NOW, DARLIN', COULD YOU PLEASE JUST CHECK THE MODEL NUMBER FOR ME?

Rule #303: "Behind every great fortune lies a great crime." —Honore de Balzac

In 1973, I was a young, starving screenwriter, and since my writing did not seem yet to warrant financial remuneration from the scions of Hollywood, I had to find a way to make a living. And so I went to work in a boiler room run by a charming but disheveled slob named "Lucky" Louie Gordon.

A boiler room is nothing more than a rat's warren of small cubicles, each padded with carpet on the walls and with a phone on a small desk. The boiler room got its name from C. H. Spurgeon, the "prince of preachers," who preached the Baptist gospel 24/7 in revival prayer meetings. As many as 5,000 people attended the meetings, which were often held in the basements of large public buildings. Steam was the power source of the day, and boiler rooms were where the vast machines and pistons were housed. Spurgeon saw his prayer services as the spiritual power to raise Christianity to a higher place—out of the basement.

Our boiler room was totally ecumenical. Its god was money. The prayer service was the scam perpetrated on the unsuspecting. In my little rat's nest, the job was simple. Move as much copy paper and Xerox toner as humanly possible across the entire United States. You can never have too much paper and toner on hand, just in case.

I would get up at 4:30 a.m., and by 5 a.m., I was at my desk working the phones. You started at 5 a.m. on the West Coast because with the time zones it was 8 a.m. on the East Coast. You just worked your way across the country as the sun rose and headed toward California. Banks started answering the phones at 9 a.m.

The pitch was simple. You called up, and a secretary/receptionist answered.

"This is Colonel Paul Biegler (my nom de plume) calling long distance. [Long distance implied that it was an important call. Remember, this is 1973.] I'm calling about your regular shipment of paper and toner for your copy machine. [Key concept here is the phrase 'regular shipment'—everything in the normal course of business. No need to make a decision.] Could you check the model number for me?" [With the model number, we could determine what the machine was and know to send the correct toner. There were a dozen major manufacturers.] Then some small talk, chat her up, how is your Uncle Harry, and then the close. "So we'll be sending just [key word here is "just"] the usual six cases, and yes, of course the 20 reams of paper. And of course, we'll just mark the paperwork to your attention, OK, Betty?"

You had to get an answer here. There was no order without some acknowledgement. After you got the approval, it was "Have a lovely day and talk to you again in a couple months, darling." Goodbye, good luck, and ring the bell.

It doesn't matter whether you are selling shit on Wall Street or shit on Robertson Avenue in Los Angeles. The cycle, the sequence, and the ring the bell are the same.

Then a day later, someone else in the company would verify the order with the woman, simply confirming the mailing address, etc. The call would be taped so when the bank manager screamed that Betty never ordered toner and paper, we could play back the tape and confirm that she actually approved the order. Some people got angry and sent the crap back to us and didn't pay. But a lot of people did.

Now if we had been sending bottles of branded Xerox toner (you know the real stuff, after all, Xerox is a registered brand name) instead of the off-brand generic junk we bought from some crazy, equally crooked company in Texas, maybe we would have a semilegitimate leg to stand on. But in addition to the generic stuff, we also charged the customer ten times more than it would normally cost. How else could they pay us the unconscionable commissions? Think about it. Commissions can be paid because the price you pay is high enough to justify it. Insurance, cars, health care, financial instruments. The list is endless. It is the American Way.

And I was good at selling this stuff. Very good. Like any actor, I got into the part and created an entire persona: a Southern WASP gentleman, Colonel Paul Biegler, named after the attorney in *Anatomy of a Murder* (Ionesco and The Bald Soprano redux). And through charm, charisma, and chicanery, I managed to unload a large amount (I believe the proper term is "shitload") of toner and paper.

Colonel Biegler went through the southeastern part of the United States like Sherman through Atlanta. I would use this big, blue book called the Bank Book. It contained the name, phone number, address, officers, branches, etc., everything you could ever want to know about that small bank in rural West Virginia with two tellers who somehow would absolutely need six cases of toner—enough to last 18 years at the rate they made copies.

Let's be really clear here. I am not proud of this adventure in the skin trade. It was a way to pay the bills so I could write screenplays and direct the Great American Movie.

It is the same hustle today. The only difference is that instead of the Bank Book, it is the Internet.

Rule #286: People in glass houses should not throw stones. Or they should have Lexan windows.

By 10 a.m. I was gone, back to my one-room apartment writing scripts for the maw of television. And that was the gig five days a week. It wasn't the *Lost Weekend* but all I had was a typewriter and a fry pan. There was no such thing as word processing in 1973. My college graduation gift had been an IBM Selectric.

The boiler room was good money. I earned about $400 per week, and my rent was $139 per month. I was definitely ready for my close-up, Mr. DeMille.

One day, a well-dressed young kid walks into the boiler room carrying an ice chest. And in the cooler are Grade A USDA steaks. Eat your heart out, Smith and Wollensky. These were gorgeous.

He tells us that he is working his way through school and he gets the steaks from his Uncle Tommy, a butcher downtown. The uncle gives the kid a couple dozen to sell each day and hey, would any of you guys want to buy some great steaks?

The kid takes the lid off the cooler and sure enough, there on top are two of the most gorgeous cows you have ever seen.

"How much?"

"Sixty-five dollars, but this is my last stop so I'll let them go for $50."

"How many in the cooler?"

"Twelve."

OK, I can do the math. That is $4.16 per steak. Each steak is a little over a pound. So rounding error included, that is about four bucks for a $15 steak. Prime steak at hamburger prices.

The magic words—*I am there for you, baby*—and I hand the kid a 50 and take the cooler. End of story.

Not exactly. I get home to my hovel, 1929 Whitley Avenue, apartment 203, complete with a Murphy bed and a view of the dumpster in the alley. Above me in apartment 303 lived a Swedish hooker who worked every night on a bed that creaked. You try being 27 years old, listening to the bouncing and the creaking of the springs on that bed every night. The thought crossed my mind more than once, but no, I was never able to close that particular deal. I had read *Catcher in the Rye*—hell, I *was* Holden Caulfield, but this was Hollywood and there were no ducks in winter.

I open the cooler, and start to put the steaks away. Hello and welcome to boiler room redux.

The top two steaks were very nice. But the remaining 10—the ones packaged under the top two—were dark gray with little white spots. Not quite with maggots yet, but they were clearly not edible.

The con had been conned. You gotta love America.

Rule #177: If a deal is too good to be true, then look for the gray steak. There is always at least one in every box.

It is a rule I have never forgotten.

Whenever I am sure I have gotten the best deal of all time on something, I always pause for a moment and look under the top steak. The gray ones are always there. You just have to look for them.

CHAPTER 16

596,000 PEOPLE WORK FOR THE UNITED STATES POST OFFICE. THERE ARE 36,400 POST OFFICES IN THE U.S. THEY LOSE THE MAIL REGULARLY. BUT THEY FOUND US.

Now Lucky Louie was a bit on the cheap side. And after about five months at his shop, I had figured out the financials of the business. It was clear that Louie was making some serious money. So I went to see the big guy in the back room and politely indicated that since I was the #1 salesman I should get a better commission split. In other words, you cheap shit, you need to pay me more. Nothing new here.

Louie, you gotta love him, looked me in the eye and told me to die and pound sand. Nothing new there either.

So I told him to go fuck himself. Nothing new either place.

Then I quit and the next week partnered up with a 22-year-old kid, G.S., who was salesman #2 and worked there as well. We rented an empty warehouse and set out to compete with Lucky and try to beat his brains in. It was strictly business.

And we did just that. We crushed him.

Rule #220: Treat your superstars well. If not, they may leave and take your universe with them.

Over the next 18 months, G.S. and I built a fairly big operation, to the point where each Friday night, we would meet in the upstairs office around 6 p.m., write each other a check for $1,500, and then go out to dinner. We had 20 employees, and we were moving the ball.

I could see the black eyes of J. P. Morgan staring down at me from the famous photo by Alfred Stieglitz. Capitalism at its best. Gordon Gecko was alive and living large in Santa Monica, California.

We were rolling. A few of my scripts were being optioned, and life was good. And then the phone rang. On a Monday at 1:30 p.m.

It was a charming gentleman from the post office. You know, the United States Post Office—the same post office that we were using to send this crap all over the United States. He could not have been nicer but he suggested in no uncertain terms that we were under consideration for indictment for mail fraud. Something about illegally transporting unordered goods across state lines.

Huh. "You must have the wrong number, sir."

"No, I don't have the wrong number. I would like to come down this week and chat with you boys."

"Sure, Friday would be just fine."

And three days later we were gone. Closed. Empty. Vanished.

Just like Redford and Newman in *The Sting*, we dismantled everything and disappeared. No cubicles, no phones, no warehouse, no boxes of paper and toner, nothing, nada, gone. Goodbye and good luck.

It had been a hell of a run but let's tell the truth. Maybe it was not actually illegal to prey on another person's lack of sophistication and greed. After all, used car salesmen do it all the time, but it was way too close to the line and I would never do it again.

When I stand in front of the pearly gates, and God asks me if I want justice or mercy, no contest. Mercy wins every time.

And I never came close to that line ever again.

Why do bank robbers always get caught? Because they always think the other guy will get caught—not them.

Rule #167: They always get caught. That is why civilization works so well.

The applicability of Rule #167 never ceases to amaze me. It doesn't matter if it is a financial Ponzi scheme or cheating on your wife, you will get caught. That is the inevitable and inexorable rule of the jungle.

It's why they make movies like *White Heat* (James Cagney), *Al Capone* (Rod Steiger), *Scarface* (Al Pacino), and *Bonnie and Clyde* (Warren Beatty and Faye Dunaway).

CHAPTER 17

"A MAN WITH MONEY IS NO MATCH AGAINST A MAN ON A MISSION"

(DOYLE BRUNSON, POKER CHAMPION)

Rule #87: When holding pocket aces, do not play your cards as if they were off-suited three and eight.

This issue of card playing pervades the entrepreneurial landscape. All negotiations, and in fact all deals, have a starting point similar to the rules of Texas Hold 'Em.

There is the deal, there is the small blind, the big blind, three rounds of betting, uncertainty, odds, bluffing, and then finally the "all-in."

I would like to make a distinction between gambling and card playing. Gambling is betting on something over which you have only modest, if any, control such as in craps, horse racing, the point spread in sporting events.

Card playing is making the most of what you have, and the outcome is one over which you have significant, if not complete, control.

Let's look at two scenarios: one in which you hold pocket aces, and one in which you have dreck.

Recently I was asked to advise a young man about his future. I think there may be a business in guiding lost souls under the age of

30 but since they won't trust anyone over 40 (which is the new 30), I don't think the idea scales.

Here are the facts. Mort is 25, has been working for six months for a start-up with a very controlling CEO. The young man is very good at what he does, which is Internet marketing. In fact, he qualifies as a superstar in his category.

The CEO moves the company from San Diego to San Francisco in order to be closer to the flow of money, talent, and technology in the Silicon Valley culture. It is important to the CEO that the company be located in the heart of the action.

(There is always an equal argument that it might be easier to build a great company in a less obvious location, e.g., Gateway Computers in Sioux City, Iowa.)

The superstar says to the CEO, "I don't want to move to San Francisco. I like it here in San Diego. I like to ride my bike and work out for my triathlons."

The CEO says, "You gotta move, you need to be part of the company and the culture, and we can build a great company but we all need to be together."

Rule #289: Hey, dude, talent rules. Follow the talent, do not force the talent to follow you. For example, Google has 67 corporate offices around the world, including 21 in the United States.

The CEO continues to pressure Mort to move, and Mort continues to resist. Tensions increase, and the conflict and total compensation are unresolved. Mort thinks he has one kind of deal, and the CEO thinks it is different. Even more troubling, the deal is still in flux.

Rule #273: Some deals are always in flux. In fact, I would suggest that in many cases, the real negotiation on a deal only truly starts after you sign what you think is the final paperwork for the deal you think you both agreed to. *But* this kind of maneuvering and positioning and circumstantial review and revisit is not appropriate for employees. It makes your employees crazy, and they will walk out the door. Employee deals need to be honored and followed not just to the letter but also the spirit of the agreement. This is true not because of litigation and human resource constraints, but because it is the right thing to do.

Rule #452: When you hold the upper hand in a lopsided negotiation where you have 90 percent of the power, be very cautious to
exercise it gently and to take care of the weaker party.

Mort comes to see me to discuss the matter, and over a period
of time I ascertain that the issue is not just money or location.
It is power and control. Mort does not like to be controlled, and
the CEO really thrives on control, even to the point of telling his
employees how to write an e-mail. That is why the CEO is insist-
ing on locating everyone in San Francisco even though the obvious
answer is to let the superstar work where he wants remotely (within
reasonable parameters).

Mort laments, "Look, just let me do my job and don't aggravate
me and continue to press me and harass me. Just let me stay in San
Diego and hit the ball. I am batting .407, I'm leading the league,
gimme a break."

The CEO continues to grind the young man and finally says,
"If you do not move to San Francisco, we will need to part ways
and find someone else. And I would like to ask you to help me hire
this person."

In effect, he fires the young man in one breath and asks him to
actively help secure his replacement in the next breath.

Rule #207: Chutzpah. It is like pornography. I can't define it, but I
know it when I see it.

What I often find lacking in young CEOs is a complete dearth
of EQ—emotional quotient. It is striking how tone deaf some
young entrepreneurs can be. I will not wander into the dark halls
of psychotherapy, but I would simply caution that developing a
very well-defined sense of EQ will enormously enhance your leadership skills and success.

The young man finally draws a line and says, "I am not going
to San Francisco."

And then the tables turn. A couple days later, the CEO calls
Mort and asks him to stay on for a few months longer, "to help us
get over this transition period, help the team, you do a really good
job, and we need more time to find your replacement."

It is right now that Mort should see that he has pocket aces. In the battle of wills, he now has a place to stand.

But Mort remains conflicted. We have several long discussions. Finally, he tells me what he really wants.

"I want to make $100,000 plus bonus in salary and commissions. I will give up my stock options (they are minimal), and I stay in San Diego, I will do my job, and I will come up to San Francisco to be part of the team five days per month. If I get that deal, I think I can hit .460. And if my batting average sinks, he can always fire me."

I suggest that he go up to San Francisco, see the CEO, and lay out his request. If the CEO says no and fires him, that is OK with Mort. And if he says yes to the package, then they have a deal.

Now what is interesting in the case is this. Mort is positive that the CEO will reject his offer. Absolutely positive.

He tells me, "Regardless of the money, look at it from his perspective. I am not willing to make the company my life. I am not willing to live and die, eat, breathe, and sleep the company. It is a job and I am not passionate about it. I like the guys, don't get me wrong, and the work is sort of interesting but generally it's mindless."

I interrupt his rant.

"Look, if he agrees to your requests, would you be satisfied?"

"Yeah, but . . ."

"No 'Yeah but . . .' Just listen. If you get what you want even though you are sure he will say 'No,' will you be satisfied?"

Pause.

Finally, the young man says, "Yes."

"Then go up to San Francisco, and tell him what you want."

This story seems simple but there is a kicker.

Rule #134: The reason that Al Pacino (you may substitute any of 25 other names here) is a great actor is because you believe he is the character. He inherits, informs, embraces, subsumes, integrates, owns the character. You believe he is Tony Montana. (Again you may substitute any of his 20 greatest movies.)

Rule #150: Do not get on the plane unless you are prepared to deliver a great performance. Seventy-three percent of negotiation is illusion. The other 27 percent is being willing to walk.

The young man had pocket aces and did not see it.

1.   He was willing to be fired. In fact he had been fired and was then asked to stay on.

2.   The issue was not money but control.

3.   The only way to stop a bully is to hit him in the nose. The only way this young man was ever going to set an even playing field with that CEO was to be willing to make a demand and stand there.

4.   I told him you don't know what you don't know. Ask the question, then shut up and wait for the answer.

5.   The guy who talks first loses.

The case ended exactly as I had suspected. Mort went to San Francisco. The CEO laid on one last guilt trip whack, our young hero followed the script (he will never be Pacino but he can probably make it in a high school production), and he got exactly what he wanted.

The story works best because he was a superstar revenue producer doing something that is currently very hard to do well. Mort is batting .490, is happy, and has been with the company beyond the six-month proposal. And he also got to keep his stock.

As a consigliore, I worry about my batting average as well. It is often the case that an outside advisor sees the facts better than the participants.

Rule #276: That is why they pay guys like Joe Torre and Phil Jackson a lot of money. Coaching is not the same as just watching the game from the bench.

But they pay the guys like Derek Jeter and Kobe Bryant even more money. Remember, the highest paid person in most companies is the VP of Sales. The guy who swings the biggest, most profitable bat should get paid the most, and if he wants to work from home or from the moon, wear pink underwear or dye his hair pink, it should not really matter.

The great CEOs know this. They make accommodations and allowances, and they encourage and support their superstars.

Remember **Rule #220:** Treat your superstars well. If not, they may leave and take your universe with them.

Our young hero almost made the classic mistake. He was sure he knew what the other guy would say before he said it. In our discussions, he would give me 20 good reasons why it would never happen. But when he stopped his own circular, self-destructive behavior and simply put on his grease paint and entered stage right, and delivered his lines with conviction, détente was achieved.

I was asked once by a middle manager what he could do to become a better "closer." I suggested to him that he might profit by taking some improv classes. The fellow was pretty straight and his ability to "bounce" a bit, to be spontaneous, to pick up verbal and physical cues, was modest.

I think all young entrepreneurs could benefit from a few classes in method acting. Lee Strasberg, who founded the Actor's Studio in New York City in 1951, is called the "father of method acting." He is the man who made Marlon Brando's shriek of "STELLA!" world famous. He trained the best of the best—Brando, Dean, Monroe, Newman, Pacino, and De Niro.

If you are going to negotiate, if you are going to represent yourself, if you are going to become what you are not yet but want to be, then you need to be believable. You need to own the role. You need to believe in your own inner life and make the audience—or whoever sits across from you—feel the commitment, the intensity, and the tensile strength that cannot be overcome or overwhelmed.

You need to be the ball.

CHAPTER 18

THE OATMEAL COOKIES ARE TO DIE FOR

Rule #284: Listen to the words, but more importantly, focus on the meaning behind them.

I started Atcom with seven employees in a two-story funky loft space in downtown San Diego, catty-corner from a small deli called The Cheese Shop.

On the first day of our new adventure, I walked across to The Cheese Shop and asked to speak to the owner, Tom Shutz. I was careful not to go during the peak lunch hour. The girl at the front went to get him, and he came out from the back to speak with me. I explained that I was the CEO of a new software company across the street and that I would like to get a charge account so that my genius engineers will not waste any time going out to get food. They can just order a sandwich, pick it up (maybe you would even deliver to us?), and that way they could keep coding. Seemed logical to me. "I would like to open a charge account."

Tom: "We don't do charge accounts."

Neil: "No, no, see you don't understand. I have these geniuses across the street, and we could give you a lot of our business because you would be the closest and easiest place to eat and so it is obviously in your best interest (think Daniel Kahneman) to give us a charge account, because it would increase your business."

Tom: "Very interesting. We don't do charge accounts."

Neil: "No, see you don't understand."

Tom: "No, kid, you don't understand. We don't do charge accounts."

Clearly, we had what is famously called "a failure to communicate."

Rule #231: "No" is just a speed bump on the road to "Yes.

I went back across the street, walked upstairs to my office, took out my checkbook, and wrote a check for $1,000 made out to The Cheese Shop. Then I walked downstairs, crossed the street, stepped gingerly into The Cheese Shop, and asked to speak to Mr. Shutz. After a couple of minutes, he came back out, with that look: You again? Go away kid, you bother me.

Before he could throw me out on my ass, I handed him the check. There was a pause, he studied it, then he studied me.

And then in a humble, soft tone of voice (no upside in being an arrogant prick), I asked, "Would it be possible to get a turkey club and open a charge account?"

Tom: "You want mustard or mayo?"

In the first interaction, Tom was not saying that he didn't do charge accounts. What he was saying was, "I don't know who the hell you are and am concerned I will not get paid."

What I gave him was not money. What I gave him was comfort. One thousand dollars worth of comfort. It was my demonstration of good faith.

Nota bene: I have been one of the longest charge account customers in The Cheese Shop history: 16 years.

And here is the kicker.

Rule #337: When The Cheese Shop bill comes into my office, it is paid within 24 hours. (The sister shop in La Jolla is owned by Tom's brother, Phil.)

It is the only bill that is paid that timely. I understand float and other people's money and leverage and negotiation as well as anyone, but I also know that an army travels on its stomach. When I am waging war, I want soldiers who have eaten well.

So, we each got what we wanted. It was just a matter of my listening to what he was really saying.

The food at The Cheese Shop is spectacularly good and fairly priced. What more could you ask for? When you go there, be sure to try the oatmeal cookies; they are to die for. I have been trying to get Phil (Tom's brother in La Jolla) to let me license the patent to the recipe, but with no success. It's a shame. Those cookies . . . he's leaving millions on the counter.

CHAPTER 19

GOOD ADVICE IS NEVER A COMMODITY

Rule #255: If you think the service you provide is a commodity, then you have diminished its worth and cannot properly value it. If your customer thinks it is a commodity, then you have no pricing power and are in a terrible business.

I recently spent 90 minutes at Osteria Romantica, a nice Italian restaurant in La Jolla Shores, talking to two of my clients. These guys are very senior managers in a major money management/ wealth management company. And the problem they were lamenting was this: How can we get more customers, and by extension, make more money?

Rule #224: The question should not be, how can we get more customers? It should be, how can we get better customers?

Here is the issue. Jim and Rob work at ABC (not the real names) and provide wealth management services. What that means is they seek out high net worth individuals and try to convince them to put their assets under management with ABC. And they try to persuade the client that if he gives Jim and Rob assets to manage, then really good things will happen for the client and Jim and Rob will mange that money better and thus make more money for the client and increase the client's net worth (as well as their own). All you need to do is pick ABC, instead of one of "those other firms," such as Goldman Sachs, Morgan Stanley, UBS, Merrill Lynch.

(There is no shortage of guys peddling financial advice. There also seems to be no shortage of wealth to manage. As a matter of fact, no one firm has more than 2 percent of the total wealth management business that is estimated to be about $3 trillion.)

When we baby boomers die, there is going to be a major transfer of wealth with a lot of dough going to our kids, many of whom will be ill prepared to deal with daddy and mommy's millions. And I assure you, before the obituary is printed, the phone is going to ring with condolences and a genuine heartfelt offer to provide some comforting financial advice. You might say one part of their business is prospecting for rich corpses.

When I sold my first technology company, the sale was reported in the paper at $70 million, and all of a sudden, out of the blue, my phone rang. After all, I was the CEO, so I must have made more than $12. Ten calls. And they all wanted to help me manage my money. They wanted to meet and go out to lunch and convince me that they could manage the money better, that the returns would be better, that they could beat the S&P or the Dow or the NASDAQ or that they could set up a hedged beta reverse spin index off the weighted average of yadda yadda. Clearly this was total unmitigated bullshit.

Rule #309: Never bullshit a bullshitter.

If I had called any one of these firms, prior to the sale, I would not have gotten the time of day. Not one chance that any of them would have taken my call. I was ugly the day before, but on 9-9-99 (the day of the sale), I had suddenly become gorgeous, I was desired, I was told I was brilliant, and I was being dressed up as prime, Grade A beef, suitable for the master cleaver. (I would have been quite happy with a pastrami sandwich.)

I agreed to meet with three of the 10. But the truth is I couldn't tell them apart. Blue suit, white shirt, nice tie. They all looked the same, and they all sounded the same. Maybe wealth management is a commodity.

Rule #182: If you want my assets, don't convince me that you will outperform the benchmark averages. Convince me that you will take care of me, that you will love me, and that I will be first among equals.

I told Jim and Rob that the close is never about beating the S&P by 8 basis points. Don't give the client charts. The close is always about an empathic connection that bridges all the fears, all the mistrust, all the small child, "Will I be safe with you?" feelings that no one in their right mind would ever verbalize at the risk of being locked up in a looney bin, but which all of us have played with in some dark, sad, lonely, scared place.

Because, sweetie, if you could really consistently outperform the averages, then you would not be hustling wealth management services. You would be running a private hedge fund; the kind of fund I can't get into because I don't have enough money.

Rule #250: Look at the cover page before you hand me the book.

So I agree to take my first "Let us manage your newfound wealth" meeting, and two charming, well-coiffed people, one man and one woman, are sitting in front of my cheap desk and they are espousing the following mantra:

"You are special to us, we will take care of you, you matter to us, it is about you, we provide personalized service, tailored to meet your every need. For now, for your future and for your generations to come, we are the team you can depend on."

The only thing they didn't say was "We're there for you, baby."

And then they handed me the investment book that lays out their qualifications and explains the asset allocations that will put me in a private jet. And I open the first page—page one, numero primo—and it says: "PREPARED EXCLUSIVELY FOR BOB JOHNSON."

This is a true story.

They were giving me the same piece of shit they had given to someone else earlier in the day. They had not even bothered to change the cover page.

You gotta love America.

I told Jim and Rob that the three most important things in one's life are wife, children, and money—followed closely by sex and religion. The rest is only commentary.

So quality money management is not a commodity. It matters greatly and it is an honorable profession. But no one in their right mind picks a manager solely on beating some benchmark average by a couple basis points. It is about the intangible issue of trust. And finding the key to that puzzle is solving the key to getting better clients.

Rule #347: Your best friends are still the guys from high school.

I was extremely lucky in one respect with regard to money. In my high school senior class, there was a very smart, somewhat strange fellow by the name of Robert Goldfarb. "The 'Farb" was unique. We all knew it. And we all knew that he was operating in a different galaxy far, far away.

Mine was a tiny high school in St. Louis, Missouri, called St. Louis Country Day School. It was an all-boys private school, mostly WASP, except my class that was a bit odd. Out of 51 students, 14 were Jewish. There must have been a mismatch in the admission algorithm that year, because this percentage never had happened previously and has never happened again.

This was the early '60s and true to form, we all got drunk (St. Louis is the home of Anheuser Busch), we inhaled, some of us got laid, we graduated, and all of us went to college; the usual dose of Harvard, Yale, and Princeton, as well as the lesser lights. No one went to Stanford. Growing up in the Midwest, it was assumed that you would go east. The west was still wild and might fall into the ocean with a mild earthquake that we were told was coming. Soon.

Goldfarb went to Yale and Harvard Business School and then he went to Wall Street, and when he was 24, he went to work for one of the most famous money managers of that era: Bill Ruane, of Ruane Cunniff.

Rule #275: Whenever possible, get a great mentor. Repeat after me: Get a great mentor.

In my senior class there was a guy named Richard Grote. His dad was pretty strong, he owned some kind of a steel mill, and they lived in a big house on a few acres in Ladue. Dick was All Everything, every sport, every party, everything. He was one of the coolest guys in the class, a wonderful, charming guy and somehow he and I became friends. I got to hang with "The Groteman" and thus got carried along like flotsam and jetsam as part of the whole cool gang. I was the token Jew taking a ride down the Nile with the Egyptians.

When I was 24, my grandfather died and left me $16,000. Dick and I had remained good friends and I called him to discuss this. After all, he was rich. We chatted for a bit and he said recently he had sent The 'Farb some money to manage.

That sounded perfect to me, so I took $4,000 I had saved plus the $16,000 I had inherited (89 percent of my net worth) and sent it to Bob along with those magic words, "Please take care of me."

Now I told you that The 'Farb was a bit strange. Here is the deal I had to make with him in order to get him to take my money. I was only allowed to call him twice a year. That's all, no more, only two times per year. And on those calls, you NEVER were allowed to ask, "So what do you think of the market?"

If you met Warren Buffett before he was Warren Buffett, would you know it?

For the first four years of the relationship, I did not make one call. I was saving them up, just in case. It is now 2011, and I have been a client of Robert Goldfarb for 41 years. Per our deal, I am entitled to 82 phone calls. I have only used 27. And I am going to continue to save them—just in case.

At the end of 41 years, the original $20,000—not including any other money sent to him, just the first monies—has turned in to $1,843,404 as of the August 2010 statement.

The 'Farb became wealthy and famous. Only in America can you find Warren Buffett masquerading as your high school class-mate. And from our class, Grote and I were the only ones who ever sent him money.

Now you tell me, is wealth management a commodity?

THERE ARE 423,491 GOLF JOKES ON GOOGLE

(THIS ONE ISN'T LISTED THERE)

I play golf with a fascinating fellow named Kent Smith. He is from North Carolina, a good old Southern boy with a steel-trap mind and a fierce commitment to golf and the Tar Heel basketball team.

He is also rich, charming, and burdened by an extreme sense of honor and integrity. For example, he does not use the foot wedge when playing golf and actually counts every stroke. Every single one!

Recently, he told me a story that I found fascinating and revealing. It came up because of a discussion about wealth managers.

It seems that Kent is a member of a group of about 20 people who, at the beginning of the professional golf tour season, each contribute $100 into a pool. They have a complicated betting system that depends on picking various players and where they finish in the four major golf tournaments: Masters, PGA, U.S. Open, and British Open.

I cannot explain the calculations (their scoring system has been known to require access to the U.C. San Diego Super Computer to determine the final outcome), but at the end of the run, $2,000 goes to one winner.

So here is his story, as best I can recount it without a North Carolina twang.

"I have a couple friends from high school, guys I have been friends with for 35 years, I mean really good friends—you know, Thanksgiving dinners, and Christmases and children—I mean longtime friends. And one of them is in our golf pool, and he invites into the deal five of his friends, so the total owing from my friend and his friends is $600. The season ends and someone else wins the dough and I contact my friend and I remind him that it is time to settle up and he has not yet put in his $600. He says, 'What do you mean 600? I only owe $100.' I tell him that those others were his friends, and he is responsible for them, and in order to make the pot right, we need $600 from you and your boys. And my friend, my friend of 35 years, says no, he isn't going to do that. He says, 'That is not my problem.' He says he will send in his $100 but the others he vouched for and brought into the deal, they are not his problem.

"So I tell him that the way I see it, it is his problem and that this is pretty important to me, and I think he ought to send the dough. And the friend declines my most polite and gracious suggestion."

So Kent writes a personal check for $600 and sends it in. The man has to make the pot right.

We finish our round and at the bar, he tells me the kicker.

"So remember I told you that this was a friend of mine of 35 years, and he was working at Oppenheimer, and he was managing some of my money. So I called him up and told him that I was disappointed in his behavior and then I closed my account with him and took back my $3 million that he was managing and put it elsewhere."

Huh! Are you telling me your friend, who was managing your money and who was getting fees for managing your money, did not see the potential consequences of his actions?

Let's take a Rational Man Behavior look at this on behalf of his friend.

1. It was $600.

2. You were managing $3 million. Let's assume a fee structure of .75 percent on assets under management. That would be about $22,500 per year in fee income.

3. You had not been doing such a good job with Kent's money anyway. (Kent had told you a couple times over the past few years that he was not thrilled with the returns you were generating, but he had hung in there with you. After all, 35 years is a long time.)

4. Paying the money was the right thing to do. You were responsible for the $600. The other five were your friends.

5. Would you rationally put at risk a friendship of 35 years and fees of $20,000 plus per year for six hundred bucks whether you thought you owed it or not?

6. Did you ever read Kahneman? You know the stuff about acting in your own best-perceived self-interest? Did you read Ariely on predictably irrational behavior?

7. In other words, *What the fuck were you thinking?*

Rule #321: Why is it so easy to see crazy, insane, stupid behavior in others and so hard to see it in ourselves?

It is this rule that keeps the psychiatric community alive and well.

What I like most about Kent's story is that in his mind, his decision flowed irrevocably from a simple set of beliefs and actions, attitudes and consequences. You did A, and I did B.

He did not call the guy to discuss or threaten or explain. He just moved his dough and never spoke to him again.

Elegant.

I love Kent Smith.

CHAPTER 21

WHY DO THEY CALL IT "CUSTOMER SERVICE"?

(IT STINKS. IT SHOULD BE CALLED "BEND OVER AND GRAB YOUR ANKLES")

Rule #65: The rats are running the renewal business.

I subscribe to *The Wall Street Journal*, and other than the editorial page, I read all four sections almost religiously each day.

I renew my subscription as it comes due. I have been a good, long-term, and loyal customer, and when I get a renewal form in the mail that says $7.60 per week, I take out a small pocket calculator and determine that the annual amount is $395.28

Are you out of your mind, Rupert Murdoch? What are you smoking—and are you inhaling?

So I call up the WSJ and say I would like a less expensive rate, and the guy on the phone tells me the following:

"The renewal we sent you is the starting point and of course I could get a cheaper rate, but we cannot give you the cheaper rate today because there are still several months left to go on your current subscription. But as your subscription gets closer to expiring, then we will give you a better rate because by then we are worried that you might cancel." Murdoch, please stop this crazy behavior. Why are you trying to screw your best customers? I read it, I pay for it, I like it (except for you and the editorial page), and you want to try to take advantage of me. Why?

What kind of customer service is this?

Offer the lousiest, most expensive rates to your best customers, assuming or hoping that they will just keep renewing without asking for a better deal because we assume you are already offering your best customers the best rate (that would be Rational Man Behavior) until one day they actually look at the renewal form. Then they get pissed off, and they threaten to cancel and then you try to bring them back into the fold by offering them a rate that is half of what you offered earlier.

Is this any way to run a business?

So, Rupert, don't bother sending me a special deal when this term runs out. See ya!

Rule #327: If you act illogically, stupidly, and venally, your customers will eventually figure it out, and they will leave you.

You may think the above story is only applicable to *The Wall Street Journal*. Wrong. It applies to every single publication with which I've dealt.

Recently, I got a renewal notice from *The New York Times*. It was for $225 per quarter. That is $900 per year, so I asked my assistant to call up and ask for a better rate. She called and they said that was the best rate they could do. So my assistant tells them that Mr. Senturia is cancelling, thank you very much, and then and only then does the lady on the other end knock $75 from the quarterly rate. That would bring it to about $600 per year.

But if I go online and subscribe to the home delivery edition, seven days a week, I get a rate of $7.69 per week, which is advertised as 50 percent off the stated rate.

OK, boys, just tell me, what the fuck is the rate? Why are there 23 different rates depending on how stupid I am?

Why do you market to the customer in a way that rewards his trust and loyalty by leading him like a dumb sheep to slaughter, assuming that he is willing to be fleeced and screwed over and treated like a lamb chop, until finally he sees the blade and bleats for a better rate?

Now that I have the lower rate, I also now know that you are rats and do not treat the customer with decency and honor and so now I will question every bill, and I will grind you and work you until eventually you pay me to take the damn paper.

And the same is true for magazines. They send two-year renewal forms every 90 days, again basing their marketing on the hope that you are stupid and will keep sending money so that you will keep getting *Newsweek* until 2029.

As a matter of fact, it is *Newsweek*'s unfunded liabilities, in part the obligation to continue to send the magazine to people from whom they have taken money for the next 15 years, that makes the sale of *Newsweek* more problematic. (The magazine recently sold for one dollar and assumption of liabilities to Sidney Harmon.)

Rule #41: Why take a good customer and turn him into a suspicious, untrusting consumer who no longer believes in you, your product, or your supposed customer service—just because you can?

To *The New York Times* and to *The Wall Street Journal*: what if you called me up and said, "You have been a good customer for 10 years, and as a way of showing our appreciation we are sending you a red whatever gizmo and also giving you, without you having to ask, beg, threaten, cajole, or rant, a discounted rate on your renewal because we want to acknowledge that we have changed our ways and are no longer going to assume that you are as dumb as a rock."

If you did that, boys, do you think you would have a customer for life?

CHAPTER 22

WHY IS APPLE STOCK AT $300 PER SHARE?

(ONE ANSWER: CUSTOMER SERVICE)

Rule #243: Do you actually think your customer is stupid or do you just treat him that way?

I own a 2002 Thunderbird, which has been serviced for most of its eight years by Mossy Ford, a well-known dealership in San Diego.

It came time to have a 35,000-mile check-up (I mostly drive it only on Sundays with the top down) and I took it to them to get an estimate. They told me it needed brakes, tires, rotors, whatever, and the total bill would be $1,900. So I said that seemed a bit expensive. Could you cut me some slack? And they said, die and pound sand.

So I went elsewhere and had all the work done for $1,350. I was thrilled. Good service, excellent work, great feeling. They were there for me, baby.

Nine days later. I come home and find a letter from Mossy Ford; a pre-printed form letter that says the following:

"According to our service file, on your last service visit, it was recommended that the following services be performed on your 2002 Ford Thunderbird." The letter lists brakes, tires, rotors, etc., exactly the items on which they'd given me an estimate.

And at the bottom of the letter is a coupon for 15 percent off all repairs and a *special discount* for the brakes and rotors from the usual $199 to $99.

You guys are so dumb it hurts.

Let's do the math: The original estimate was $1,900. If you then gave me the 15 percent discount, that gets it to $1,615 and then you knock off the extra $100 for the brakes, and the final bill would have been $1,515. If you would have offered me that discount two weeks ago, I would have gladly agreed, and it would have been a done deal.

Now I have gone elsewhere and will never come back—and not because your work is shoddy. Your work is fine. It is your customer service and pricing that assumes I am a total jerk and should be screwed repeatedly like a lug nut.

Think about this: No discount and then less than two weeks later, great discount. In the interim? Lost customer. Good bye.

Why is it so difficult to practice Rational Man Behavior? Think of the cost of customer acquisition. It is always harder to get a customer back. You never want to lose a customer once you have him. Never let him get to the door and look for an alternative. You may be very surprised at what he finds.

CHAPTER 23

"GO DOWN, YELTSIN, WAY DOWN IN RUSSIA LAND, LET MY PEOPLE GO"

(WITH AN APPROPRIATE CREDIT TO MOSES)

"Hello. My name is Mart, as in Wal-Mart. Please get on the bus."

Rule #319: Entrepreneurship is alive and well in Estonia.

Just to set the stage, Estonia is no Russian technology backwater. Skype was started by three young geniuses from Estonia. The information technology services business in Estonia is booming. Fortune 100 companies have located offices there. Technical entrepreneurship is thriving. Estonia is the most wired country in the world with 97 percent Wi-Fi coverage—and *it's all free.*

But while that kind of entrepreneurship is an easy one to focus on, there is another, even more virulent kind. It is found in the spirit of a country that got its independence from Russia 20 years ago and has not looked back, even for a moment. This is a country and a people who are passionately embracing personal expressions of freedom and individual explorations of capitalism.

Welcome aboard the kayak trip to Pedassaare Island in Estonia with Mart as your guide and leader.

Mart is 6'3" with a mane of curly, blonde hair and an athletic build. Basically he is gorgeous with a big personality. While the bus drove us out to the launching point, Mart gave us a one-hour talk about Estonia and its history. He was knowledgeable and proud of his country, and one comment struck me squarely. "Estonians do not like laws." Given their long history of being dominated by Russia and others, Estonians are not big fans of government mandates. Mart says, "We have rules," but he made the distinction between that which is legislated and dictated by government (laws) and that which grows organically and is accepted by all the people (rules).

The people are rebellious at being controlled. (You would be too, if someone had been telling you what to do for 800 years.)

What has evolved over the last 20 years is a series of rules and behavior evolved by the citizenry and codified not as laws per se, but as accepted practice. Rational agreements of the people, by the people, and for the people. Fascinating. It is a country's embrace of Rational Man Behavior.

Estonia got its independence in 1991. Mart was born in 1975 so his perception of unlimited personal opportunity was not colored by the previous 800 years of Russian/German/Danish/Swedish domination.

Estonia is the poster child for a people who hate being controlled. A true country for rebels with a cause. (You can understand then how quickly I signed up for an Estonian summer house.)

When we got to Mart's operation at the lake, there were 25 kayaks neatly arranged and ready to go. The trip out and back was marvelous including lunch and a torrential downpour. But, hey, we were in kayaks, so getting wet was not really an issue. We were already soaked.

At the end, over a fireside beer, I asked him who owned the kayak operation. Did he like working for the company? At first, he was a bit shy about the answer but then he proudly confessed that he and two other buddies of his had begun the service three years ago.

They had started with two kayaks. Now they had 25. They had built their own business. Entrepreneurship had reared its wet head. At the beginning, their customers were the locals but they quickly figured out that the perfect customers were the luxury cruise line passengers. They reached out to the top tier, Regent, Windstar,

Silversea, Crystal, and became the premier provider of the kayak excursion to Pedassaare Island. And business boomed.

Mart had his kayak business in the summer months. In the winter, he taught at the university and provided outdoor guiding services for hunters and hikers.

He was quite proud that the television show, *The Great Race*, had come to Estonia to film an episode, and he had been hired as the local liaison. Given my previous travails in that slough of despond, I was sympathetic to the story of his "hassle with Hollywood."

It was classic *Day of the Locust* meets *Sunset Boulevard.*

The television director hires Mart, and on the first day of shooting, out in the middle of nowhere, in a swamp-jungle setting, the director tells Mart how he wants to shoot this difficult stunt. Mart advises the director that the way he has staged it is too dangerous, completely unsafe.

The director proceeds to make clear to Mart that he, the director, is in charge and that this is what he wants the shot to be. Mart is an imposing fellow physically and suggests again to the director that his idea is not a good one, and that it is simply too dangerous.

The director, new to Estonia and not being used to any kind of disagreement or insubordination, proceeds to make very clear to Mart that he wants what he wants and he expects to get it. After all, he is a Hollywood television director.

Mart says that he will not participate. It is too dangerous. "And further, Mr. Director, if you continue to insist, I will walk off the set."

The director is a bit taken aback, but once again makes clear his demand.

"Goodbye." Mart turns and walks away.

Now remember, there are about 20 people with cameras, lights, and equipment in the middle of a jungle.

You can guess how this ends. The director finally embraces Rational Man Behavior and begs Mart to come back. From that point on, it is very clear who was in charge. The director had clearly not read the information packet in his hotel room about rules, laws, and dictatorial behavior.

Rule #290: When in Rome, do not argue with the guy who manages the chariots.

CHAPTER 24

"YOU TALKIN' TO ME?"

(TRAVIS BICKLE, *TAXI DRIVER*)

It was October 2008. Lehman had just gone broke, and the world was embarking on a double black diamond, worldwide financial meltdown.

I had just embarked on another start-up, which turned out to be a disastrous adventure, an online news and information website. However, with no ability to see *The Black Swan*, I did not know at the time that the avalanche of incompetent hires, inadequate capitalization, an ill-conceived business plan, a bone-crushing recession that had just started were all simultaneously breaking free from the top of the mountain and were headed directly toward me. I simply assumed, also incorrectly, that I could ski out ahead of the slide.

Rule #194: No one is that good of a skier.

Eventually the online news project would end in financial loss, humiliation, and failure. Stay tuned for News at 11. It's in the next book.

One afternoon I came back from a meeting, and my assistant said an interesting fellow had just come in looking to rent two spare offices. The young man had been wandering in the neighborhood, saw the building, liked the location, had gone up to see the management company on the second floor and asked to rent space. The building is full, but they said, "Try Mr. Senturia in suite 120, he might have a spare office."

He pleaded his case to Ms. Nicole Rockstead, my administrative, global executive advisor, assistant, and general factotum for the last 18 years and without whom I would have long ago truly died and pounded sand (as I have been advised to do on more than one occasion).

I believe you can tell a lot about a person's character by asking how many secretaries/assistants they have gone through in the last five years. If the head guy is a churn 'em and burn 'em type, it tells you something. If a CEO cannot keep quality assistants, then it says something about his style—and what it says is not good.

On occasion I have been asked for personal references. I simply tell them to call Nicole. It has worked every time. I know she is valuable and am reminded of it at least two to three times per year when my business associates offer her more money and try to hire her away from me.

I listened to Nicole's rundown of the guy's pitch. Not interested. Please tell him politely to fuhgetaboutit. No room at the inn.

And she says to me, "I don't know. This was a very interesting guy. I think you should meet with him."

Nicole is my touchstone to Rational Man Behavior. So when Nicole makes a suggestion, I listen with keen interest. When Ms. Rockstead tells me to do something, there is a 98.24 percent chance that is exactly what I will do.

"Of all the gin joints in all the towns in all the world, she walks into mine." —Rick Blaine, *Casablanca*

One day later Mr. Robert Brannigan shows up in my office, ostensibly to rent a spare office. He is a handsome young man right out of central casting from the movie *Goodfellas*. He is a 27-year-old Italian, street-smart kid, charming, respectful, and polite. He makes his case for renting a couple of offices. Why does he need offices? Well, he just moved to San Diego a week ago to relocate his business from Buffalo, New York. He said he'd come to San Diego because the weather was better.

Come on, any weather is better than Buffalo's.

Rule #38: No matter what, you should always be polite.

"Sorry, I really don't have any extra space, but I wish you well."
I walk him to the elevator. As he is about to get in, I ask him:
"By the way, what is your business?"
"I have an online website that sells used textbooks."
"Nice. Any revenue?"
"Yeah."
"Great. Can you tell me how much?"
"Sure. We did $8 million last year."
"Come on back inside. We should talk."

Rule #242: Nicole knows best.

And thus began the saga of Bobby Brannigan and Valore Books. We sat and talked for two more hours. I learned that he started his little company six years before, financed its growth on credit cards, never took outside money, built it with friends he played ice hockey with at State University of New York at Fredonia. His dad was a butcher in Brooklyn. The kid had both moxie and brains. How could I resist?

Bobby was highly motivated to find a mentor. He was hungry to grow his business. He had big dreams, and he understood his business and the market ice cold. He had integrity. He said he wanted to take his company to the next level. And he meant it.

Rule #104: A lot of people talk about that next level. Talk is cheap. It requires massive commitment and a tall ladder. There are no elevators.

I became his consigliore. I helped with strategy, hiring, software, leases, financing, marketing, and business deals gone south. I guaranteed a $750,000 line of credit. I got some stock and became Chairman of the Board. I guided Bobby in his personal pursuit of excellence. I was in this company up to my waist. Bobby was in up to his neck.

What persuaded me to do the deal was that Bobby was clear about wanting to build a professional company. He wanted a big company but at his heart what he really wanted was to be a better

CEO. He had outgrown his ice hockey pals and was ready to try to build a first-rate management team.

And he was deeply sincere and aware of his own (perceived) shortcomings. He had triumphed up to this point on sheer, unmitigated desire.

Over the next 24 months, Bobby built the company to $21 million in revenue, and he is now in the process of raising money from a private equity company that wants to enter the college textbook rental and marketplace business.

Rule #73: The desire to change can only come after an awareness of the need for change.

Rule #72: When a goose wants to walk in the door, don't be so fast to close it. You won't know if it is golden until you hear him quack.

CHAPTER 25

THEY WERE YOUNG AND THEY WERE BRILLIANT

(I WANTED TO STRANGLE EACH OF THEM AT LEAST ONCE)

"I coulda been a contender. I coulda been somebody, instead of a bum, which is what I am." —Terry Malloy, *On the Waterfront*

There are times in everyone's life when you look back with a bit of regret, sometimes fond regret and sometimes bitter regret. In my case, it is more on the fond side. If I had been more rational when I was younger, if I had been a less angry young man, if I had acted in less neurotic ways, I think I could have been more successful—not just financially but in all ways: socially, emotionally, psychologically, and humanly.

Rule #302: More money is lost through neurotic behavior than through bad business decisions.

Sure, I think the private jet would have been nice. (I have flown in one a few times but will never own one.) I certainly could have had the second home in Montana for fly fishing but Rational Man Behavior argues forcibly that a second home makes no sense except in very rare instances. After the most recent real estate crash, I suspect second homes will end up being very available and only modestly desired. Besides, my wife wants to go to lots of different vacation places, not repeatedly back to Bozeman and the Madison River.

Rule #311: Sometimes you have the brass ring in your hand—and don't know it. When you look back and see it, you will wonder for a long time why you didn't recognize it when it counted.

In 2000, I started a company with four smart young men. We had the brass ring in our hands, and didn't know it. It looked like a cheap plastic toy. We got confused.

The term "brass ring" comes from a game played on the carousel. The brass ring is what you try to grab from a dispenser as you sit on the horse and go round and round. If you could hook one and hold onto it, you won a prize.

Rule #226: It's the going 'round and 'round that makes you crazy.

We had successfully sold Atcom to CAIS in late 1999, and along the way had made eight paper millionaires (out of 44 employees). The NASDAQ market was booming, and I was hungry for another deal.

After the sale to CAIS closed, I was asked to relocate to another building. The new CEO, the person who shall not be named, thought I might be a disruptive presence in the cloistered hallways, might foment revolution, trying like a deposed French king to regain the crown. The guy fancied himself Richard III (hunchback and all). Me, I was glad to get out of there.

It was Thanksgiving 1999. Nicole and I had adjourned to a two-room suite in a downtown high-rise to contemplate our navels, worry about the stock price, the lock-up terms, and figure out how to get back into the game. There was the usual deal flow, and I worked on three or four, seeing if I could find lightning in a bottle a second time.

This start-up technology business had been pretty good to a first timer. Now that I was a "been there, done that CEO," I thought the rats in Silicon Valley could not use that as an excuse not to fund me. I was wrong again.

The deal business is like trolling for marlin. Nothing. Nothing. Then, fish on.

In February 2000, I got an interesting call. A couple with whom my wife and I had been friendly and who were modest angel investors in town phoned and said they had met a brilliant undergraduate at UC San Diego who was studying computer science. He had started a website that searched for bits of source code that could be re-used elsewhere. Our friends said that he was thinking about starting a company. Would I meet with him? Can GEICO save you money on your car insurance?

We agreed to meet with him and his partners at his off-campus apartment at 8 a.m. on a Tuesday. Their classes started at 10 a.m. that day. We brought pastries and knocked on the door.

These were three very smart people—*very smart*. Sameer Samat, the leader of the gang, was tall, handsome, charming, brilliant, and well spoken. Living with him were two more young geniuses, Chris Harris and Josh Dammeier. There was a fourth member of the cabal, Sean Brady, who was a student at Cal Poly San Luis Obispo.

The four musketeers. Armed and dangerous. These kids were not Ph.D.s. They were what Ace Greenberg called "PSDs": Poor, Smart, with a deep Desire to become rich. My kind of deal.

Rule #307: Always bet on the jockey. This rule is inviolate.

These four guys had developed some very sophisticated software that was very good at data mining and search.

Huh, did I say search?

I quickly went to school to bone up on the various search algorithms—Bayesian probability and "N nearest neighbor." There were five or six companies that were knocking around in this space, and the boys had a strong solution. Google was only incorporated in 1998. There was Alta Vista and Northern Light and others. The space was not locked up yet.

The boys and I met three more times, and after some discussion about rich versus king, we settled on a deal.

Rule #392: The rich versus king principle is a simple one. Do you want to be king and in total control of your territory? Or do you want to be rich? As king, you own it all, even if the entirety of your subjects is only four people, two cows, and a dog. King is about being in charge. Or do you want to be rich? Wanting to be rich means putting the right people in the right seats, on the right bus, going in the right direction, with the right driver—even if that driver is not you. But that's OK because the good news is this: You still own a lot of the bus.

Rule #132: If there are four founders, it doesn't mean that the equity should necessarily be split equally, 25 percent each. Life isn't fair.

It was clear to me that the workloads and the contributions would be different from each of them, and I encouraged Sameer, who was the leader, to assert that leadership by taking a bit more of the equity for himself. He felt strongly, not unlike the musketeers, that it was all for one and one for all.

Normally, the all-for-one model is a disaster. In this case, and to the credit of the boys, they made it work. Sameer did carry the biggest oar but he was comfortable with the arrangement. And to their credit, not once did the ownership structure get in the way of our work.

The product was going to be a software program that did data mining and content management, and the first vertical we picked was résumés. We were going to make software that allowed companies to match résumés and jobs more effectively.

Today that is a no-brainer. In 2000, it was reasonably cool. We called the company "Mohomine," named after the famous mohorovic discontinuity. I am sure you are all familiar with this term. The discontinuity is the boundary between the Earth's crust and the mantle. The moho lies entirely within the lithosphere, and scientists believe that if you could get to the moho, this place deep in the Earth, all the secrets of the universe would be revealed.

Bottom line: We were really good at searching for stuff and categorizing the stuff we found.

Rule #209: Who you know can be really important if you know who you know.

Sameer was friends with a young man named Sergey Brin. Sergey was the co-founder of Google. During the first year of Mohomine, Sameer had a couple of conversations with Sergey. After all, they were in search, we were in search. Shop talk.

But in the end, the five of us decided that there was no money in search.

We concluded that there was no money in search.

In case you missed the last two sentences, please allow me to repeat. *The four founders and I concluded that there was no money in search.*

Please allow me to pause here while I put the gun to my head for the 50th time and consider carefully pulling the trigger, still wondering exactly how we came to such a brilliant and misguided conclusion.

I have placed that one sentence on my wall just to remind me that I don't know what I don't know, and I don't know it a lot of the time.

We had some very good search software, and we were contacted by or met with all of the pretenders to the Google throne, including Yahoo, Ask Jeeves, etc., but in the end, we couldn't find a fit, and we went on down a different road.

Interesting road, interesting journey. But we had to take the journey on foot. The private jet thing belonged to Brin and Page by then.

Toward the end of 2001, the tech world was crashing (or at least the NASDAQ was), and we spent a lot of time on Southwest Airlines flying from San Diego to San Jose going to meetings and begging.

We get to the airport, rent the car, go to Sand Hill Road, meet the Fockers, and are told that we are too early, we are too late, the market is not big enough, it's too small a deal, it's too big a deal, we need to syndicate it, we need to lead, we need seven Board seats, your management team stinks, you don't have enough revenue, your roadmap is unclear, we just funded your competitor—but come back to us when you are a little further along. And hey, your software is great, but, but, but, but . . .

We got our first customer in early 2001: PeopleSoft (since acquired by Oracle). They had a software business application suite and needed the résumé function we had created. We flew to Pleasanton, California, a few times, demoed the software, and after they had performed the standard large company technical issue proctology exam on the small company, they agreed to make a deal.

Ah, yes, the deal. The deal. We had met with their product managers, their technical team, their marketing team, their program managers, their business development team, even their lunch room busboys. We were now ready to meet the Deal Guy, the Stone Cold Steve Austin of Pleasanton.

We had batted the ball around for a couple of weeks. Offer, counter-offer. It was time to fish or cut bait. The conference call was set for noon. We were in our conference room, just Sameer and me. It was time to finally and firmly ask for the order.

Rule #83: If you don't know how deep the water is, diving in head-first is simply the triumph of terror over caution.

Somebody had to price the deal. After some pleasantries, we cut to the chase, and I asked for a $1 million upfront pre-paid royalty, along with all the other bells and whistles in a standard OEM (original equipment manufacturer) deal.

"We hear you. We will get back to you."

And just like that, the call was over. Sameer thought I was out of my mind. When the call ended, he freaked and indicated a sincere desire to strangle me, assuming that I had blown the whole deal and that his entire net worth software future was now headed directly toward the toilet. We were dead in the water, they would never do this, the number was crazy, and how did I manage to destroy his company?

Maybe he had a point. But at the time, my mantra was sit tight, they will call back—and worst case, they will counter. But, I told him, they will not walk away.

Rule #407: When simultaneously whistling and praying in the graveyard, try the tune from "Only the Good Die Young" by Billy Joel

So we waited.

Rule #110: Do not pick up the phone and call them. Do not pick up the phone. Do not pick up the phone.

Rule #179: Where you stand dramatically affects your point of view. Perspective and risk assessment are variables. It depends which end of the telescope you look through.

Let's review the bidding. Sameer was a young genius with his first company and $11 in the bank, and I was a 50-year-old business guy who had just sold his last company and was buying a new sailboat (a small one, but nonetheless).

And so we waited.

This was a stressful five days. Sameer and I were not speaking. On the last day that we were supposed to hear from PeopleSoft, the four founders came into my office at noon and suggested politely that if this deal cratered, I would be asked to leave the building by 5 p.m.

PeopleSoft called at 4:30 p.m. that day and agreed to the terms. Three weeks later, they sent a $1 million check, which I promptly took to Kinko's and blew up to six feet by nine feet and stuck on the wall.

We were alive. At least for a while longer.

CHAPTER 26

"BEHIND EVERY SUCCESSFUL MAN IS A WOMAN, BEHIND HER IS HIS WIFE"

(GROUCHO MARX)

Rule #400: Déjà vu all over again.

The Moho team was rolling along, and again I was blessed to be running a company that had world-class software as its key asset.

I was beginning to see a pattern here. In the case of Atcom, it took us two tries to find the business model that worked. Here we were in the next company, a little screwed up, but with great software and again not totally clear about our business model.

I cannot program the VCR or the thermostat. But I know great software when I see it—and I deeply and passionately love great software engineers.

During the early days of Mohomine, I faced an interesting dilemma. My assistant, Ms. Rockstead (you remember her, the one who has bailed me out of shit so many time, that I bought her a backhoe for Christmas one year) gets married—and becomes pregnant. Who would have ever thought such a thing could happen? Some nerve! Doesn't she know I am trying to run another company into the ground and I need her?

Aren't there any rules to protect neurotic, needy CEOs who can't live without? Where can I find a good human resources lawyer to represent that minority class of CEOs?

Ms. Rockstead gave birth to her baby. In her usual best form, she stopped working only three days before she delivered. And 14 days later, she was back at the office—*with the baby.*

Rule #90: When the standard solution doesn't work, create a new solution.

Nicole was given a private office, a very large corner office, and in it we put a crib, a bassinet, a hot plate, refrigerator, blankets, toys, a cot, a TV, and whatever else she wanted. And so Ms. Avalon Rockstead, three weeks old, and her mother, began work at Mohomine. We carried Avalon on the books as a 1099 contractor.

For one year, Nicole breast fed Ms. Avalon and had at her disposal 39 uncles/aunts/babysitters if she needed to nap, go out and buy something, whatever. Everyone in the company took care of Avalon. In retrospect, it was amazing. I am not sure we could ever pull this off again but for that one year, while the company was growing, it worked. Hillary Clinton said it takes a village. That seems a bit big to me, but 39 friendly, loving faces was about right.

Nicole was amazing, and Avalon thrived. She is now 10 years old and seems to exhibit no ill effects from starting her corporate life at such a young age.

Rule #163: Your key people need to be accommodated. They are very hard to replace and frankly, you don't want to replace them.

P.S. Nicole got to keep the corner office until we moved into bigger digs two years later.

CHAPTER 27

IF I TELL YOU, I WILL HAVE TO KILL YOU

For Mohomine, we had raised about $7 million in venture capital over two rounds. One of the investors that participated was most interesting and unique. It was In-Q-Tel.

In-Q-Tel was the venture investment arm of the CIA. The federal government had created it with the mission of bridging the gap between the security and technical needs of our government and the solutions being developed in Silicon Valley and other technology centers. In a nutshell, In-Q-Tel was supposed to create an inviting environment for the genius nerds in technology so they would get past their ingrained predisposition to distrust all government pinheads.

The way they were going to do it was to form a venture firm to invest in start-ups whose technology or product could be valuable to our country in multiple areas: everything from content management to bomb detection sensors to biotech to equipping the modern technology warrior in the field. The list is long. At one point In-Q-Tel had invested in over 100 companies, and the only common characteristic was that the "product" could be useful to the CIA and our government.

In-Q-Tel was charged with providing money, leadership, and access so that the daunting task of doing business with the government would be less difficult, and in the end, both our country and the company would be better for it. The brains behind this scheme was one Gilman Louie, an ex-videogame designer best known for creating the Falcon, the F-16 flight simulator. He was also the person who licensed Tetris from developers in the Soviet Union. I loved Gilman. He was my James Bond.

It was March 2002, Moho had been in business about a year, and we were making software that was used for résumé capture and search (the PeopleSoft deal) when one day the phone rings and Gilman Louie, a man I had never heard of at that time, says, "Why don't you come up to Silicon Valley and have a cup of coffee with me?"

You may remember September 11, 2001.

And thus began my multi-year association with In-Q-Tel and Gilman. It seems that the government badly needed software that could parse and categorize some obscure foreign languages, software that could "read" documents written in Pashto and Farsi (Iraqi languages). Our software was able to do that. Our software was really good at pattern recognition and content management. The war in Iraq was problematic in many ways, one of which was trying to decipher the reams and reams of documents that were being collected. The government needed to find the "intelligence" in the documents, the kernel of value in the sea of corn. There were millions of documents, and it was impossible for the individual analysts to read all of them. Our software was able to "understand," to make sense of, to "read" the Pashto/Farsi documents at very high speed. For example, a typical 250-page book could be reviewed in less than 45 seconds.

So I got a small chance to be a tiny patriot. Our government came calling and we answered. But, it was not all altruism. They also came with a check. They invested. They were customers.

I loved working for the CIA. Say what you will about government, spies, Big Brother, whatever—the bottom line is simple. I love America and was honored to be doing one tiny, small part.

Without overstating the case and making our little company out to be more than one tiny cog in a giant system, nonetheless, there was a sense that the men and women in the Agency were making decisions and relying on our software. If it failed, if it didn't work well, we were putting other people at risk. It was not just a lost e-commerce sale; it included the possibility of someone actually dying.

Rule #278: The American flag aspect does kind of put a different spin on things.

At the end of my first meeting with Gilman, who was charming and focused, I asked, "I have one question. How did you find out about us?"

"Senturia, that is a dumb question. What do you think? *We're the CIA.* We can find out anything about anybody." He smiled and from then on, he had me. I would have walked on broken glass for Gilman.

In addition to In-Q-Tel, we had two local venture firms in the deal and for a while, we rolled merrily along. We sold our software to big companies like Oracle, SAP, and PeopleSoft, and smaller companies like Kofax, and of course to the federal government.

Moho was blessed with a unique mix of technical talent. We had the four founding geniuses, all under 25, and they had the requisite Foosball, Ping-Pong, pizza, shorts and flip-flops, work until 3 a.m. culture.

We also had four brilliant geniuses from Qualcomm. They had jumped ship to try their hand at the get-rich, start-up, be-your-own boss model. They were buttoned up. The two groups made interesting bedfellows. Brilliant and buttoned versus brilliant and unbuttoned. The turf wars were incessant, the battles fierce, the technical roadmaps filled with IEDs. My "taking care of" was constant. You can't live with them; you can't live without them.

Rule #258: Nothing will prepare a CEO for working with engineering, genius, arrogant, difficult, uncommunicative, neurotic, brilliant people. Nothing!

In my first company, Atcom, we had eight engineering geniuses with the lead guy, Peter Van Horne, being very difficult. He was immensely talented, but incorrigible. Most nights I came home bruised from his constant assaults on my stupidity, my inability to lead, my incapacity to understand, my lack of skills in every area from the boardroom to financing to sales to advertising to business development. Thank God I have a strong ego or I would have killed myself. After the company was sold, he walked out a multi-millionaire, of course.

And here I was at Mohomine, again in the same Ninth Circle of Software Developer Hell.

Rule #154: "Abandon hope, all ye who enter here." —Dante Alighieri

Here is a story.

We needed a genius with a certain database skill set. It was 2002, and geniuses were in hot demand. We placed an ad and found a post-doctoral Cal Tech student by the name of Mauritius Schmidtler. He had exactly what we needed so we invited him down to San Diego from L.A. for an interview. It was a match made in heaven—or so I thought.

Mauritius was earning $32,000 working as a post-doctoral fellow for a professor. He was married and afraid to leave his job. It was nice, safe, and secure, and he and his wife, Julie, were planning on having a baby. The professor told Mauritius that if he did good work and behaved himself, then one day in the future he would have tenure, a pension, and a wonderful life.

I pointed out to Mauritius that this "future" would occur about 28 years from now and of course the professor doesn't want you to leave since you are brilliant and he needs you. But what about your current future—your now future?

Mauritius was not convinced. I offered him $75,000, plus we would move him to San Diego, and hey, I'm there for you, baby (and for his prospective baby).

But he was not quite "there." He said he had to discuss the situation with Julie. I said, "Bring Julie down, let me talk to her." I figured that if I could get time with his wife alone, I could close her.

The next week, Julie came down to San Diego with Mauritius. She was gorgeous, charming, loved her husband desperately—and it turned out that she was the risk-taker. She had just one question: What would happen if we went broke?

Rule #133: "What will happen if we go broke?" is the one question you can never really answer well. Everybody's tolerance for risk, pain, disappointment, loss, and potentially having to start over is different. Whatever your answer, you must never lie to your potential employee. Never.

I looked her in the eye. And I told her the other truth. Your husband is brilliant. He will always be able to get a job. But this might be a time when taking the risk is worth it. If it works out, the payday will be strong. If we go broke, you both will land on your feet because he has enormous talent. But no promises. We could just as easily go broke.

But, then like all CEOs, I needed to shade things just a tiny bit. "I feel very confident about our chances."

So they said yes, and now in addition to my responsibility to the employees and the investors, I also had the personal responsibility for their unborn children. But Mauritius was the key to the puzzle. A monster talent. Along with Chris Harris, he took us to a new level.

I ended up the godfather of two of their four children. He does not have tenure at Cal Tech but Julie has advised me that she is quite happy with the deal they both made.

Still, at the end of running five software/technology companies, my conclusion is that the planetary DNA of the genius developer engineer can often be antithetical to the basic Rational Man Behavior expectations of the CEO. Since I am not an engineer, it is of course possible that it might be more my problem than theirs. But I don't think so.

There is a famous software developer axiom I strongly adhere to.

What is the difference in cost between a good engineer and a great engineer? The answer is simple. The good one you pay $105,000 per year. The great one you pay $150,000. And the difference in value to your company is also simple. It is measured in multiple millions of dollars, of skills, output, creativity, problem solving, and coding elegance. The good one is worth what you're paying. Great is the best bargain going.

Rule #113: Whenever possible, hire the very best, and willingly, even enthusiastically, pay the freight.

Unfortunately, Moho got caught in a small double whipsaw and, given the recession of 2004, we could not raise another round of financing and had to sell the company.

To whom? Our biggest customers did not want to buy us because they had problems of their own. So we turned to one of our most recent customers—Kofax. Our software was a perfect complement to their core business. Kofax was owned by DICOM, Plc, a public Swiss company.

I won't bore you with the foreplay, the kiss and tell, the meeting the father, the dinner dance at the country club, the mother-in-law from hell, the best man, the rented tux, and finally the ceremony. All that was left was to argue about was the size of the dowry.

They brought their entire due diligence team to San Diego for a few days—and they worked us over. The CEO was American, and several of the key engineers and management members were Swiss-German.

You know about Swiss watches. Well, these boys were detailed to a fault. If I showed them a green piece of paper, they were not inclined to believe that it really was green until I found the paint swatch and the Pantone color chip number and got a can of it from the hardware store and showed them the paint and then painted the side of a barn so they could watch it dry to make sure it didn't turn blue after a week in the sun.

"Ja, ve have our vays."

We got to the end of the negotiations. They were buying the company for about $10 million, enough for the venture capitalists to get their dough back, and the rest of us would make enough to buy a latte.

We were down to the very fine strokes. Deal was done, except for one last item. We were arguing about the "holdback in escrow." This is a concept that says a certain amount of the purchase price money is not paid to the seller but rather is held in escrow for six to 18 months to protect the buyer just in case something the seller had promised (known as representations and warranties) turned out to be false.

This is usually heavily negotiated. The buyer wants the biggest number in escrow for the longest time, just in case. And the seller wants the smallest number and the shortest time. Give me my money and let me get out of Dodge.

The negotiations dragged on, and every time I thought we had agreed to something, they moved my cheese a little further away. And to complicate matters, our dealings were always with the American team. Then they secretly talked to the Swiss boys, who then communicated back to their own team, who then called to tell us what the guys in Europe wanted. But we had no way to deal directly with the decision makers.

Rule #42: Find out who the true decision maker is, and deal with him or her.

Sure, yeah, great, easy for you to say. You're so smart. Go fuck yourself. You are still stalled in the muck with the general manager and the Deutschland *uber alles* Chief Technical Officer.

The sticking point in the deal was the escrow holdback. They wanted 25 percent and a very complicated earn-out designed to screw us. I wanted an 8 percent holdback, more cash up front, and a very small earn-out. This principle is known as "I want all my money up front, you bastards, because I know in the end you are going to screw me blind on the terms of the earn-out, and I will never see another dime. And don't tell me the check is in the mail."

This particular negotiating nuance is taught word-for-word at some of the finest business schools in the country.

After a few weeks of back and forth, we had both taken up residence in Stalemate City. We had a cultural divide. They did not want to show any weakness to the management in Switzerland, and I was looking for Reasonable Man Behavior with no agenda. I did not need to impress anybody. The VC investors had confidence in me and had given me a lot of room to maneuver without second-guessing. I had the ball on my own 20 with two minutes to play. It would be what it would be. That vote of confidence was remarkable on their part, and I was grateful and have thanked them often.

I came up with a simple ploy. At the next negotiation I added an outrageous demand. Immediate acceleration of all employee stock, a new request that was clearly not reasonable. And I went hard to the hoop on it. I told them it was a deal point and what the hell, I might as well walk and find another buyer and who needs you and don't let the door hit you on your way out. I had drawn a line in the sand—over something that was stupid!

Rule #135: It is all about acting and performance. Make the audience believe the character. Be the character. "Stella!"

The "Ja, ve have our vays" boys went ballistic. I was accused of re-trading the deal, of bad faith, of torpedoing the U-boat. They threatened to pick up their Swiss fondue pots and their oompah band tubas and walk away.

Tense time. Reminded me of waiting for the PeopleSoft call.

Rule #388: It is OK to draw a line in the sand but be very careful about drawing one in concrete. Sand doesn't harden as quickly.

There were a series of hostile e-mails, angry lawyers, and scared employees leading to the final call.

Arnold von Buren, the DICOM CEO, makes the last call. After pleasantries, he makes an impassioned speech pointing out that my demand is unreasonable, outrageous, and could scuttle everything. (That is the whole point, my friend.)

Silence on my part. Do not speak. You know this rule.

"How can you put this whole thing at risk? We have been working on this deal for more than three months. We are ready to go. But we cannot, we will not, we simply cannot agree to the stock demand, it is a deal breaker for us."

"OK, Herr von Buren, I sincerely understand what you are saying [remember, negotiators give concessions, they do not give reasons] and in the spirit of good will and a desire to achieve a positive outcome for these two great companies [I could have been a government speech writer] I will waive my stock demand, but I think it is only fair that you agree to the 8 percent escrow holdback blah blah . . ."

He agrees and the deal is done.

Rule #272: Create something you can give away.

Put something in play in the deal that you know is crazy, hold to it, but know that it is a toss-out. When you give it up reluctantly but graciously, the other side is usually inclined to then give you the other thing that you really wanted.

Now, this seems simple but there are two puzzlers here:

1. Put the thing you will give up into the game as early as possible. (I did not do this as well as I should have.)

2. Convincing and managing the fear of the employees and your Board that you are not in fact a maniac terrorist intent on blowing up the whole thing to serve your demented ego-maniacal need to control, exert authority, demonstrate power, and dominate is a bit tricky.

Nota bene: In the end they did screw us on the escrow earn-out calculation, so the difference between 25 percent and 8 percent was worth over $1 million to the investors and employees.

And as for Swiss watches? I think they are overrated. I wear a Timex.

CHAPTER 28

RASHOMON'S REVENGE

Author's Note: I asked one of the four founders of Mohomine, Chris Harris, to share some of his thoughts and to recount his version of certain events as he perceived them. In classic Rashomon style, the following story is Mr. Harris's recounting of certain facts in the case. I think the "truth" is always elusive in many instances so I am giving you, the reader, an opportunity to be your own Akira Kurosawa and indulge in an alternate perspective from one of the principals.

"Who the hell is that? Who could possibly be ringing the doorbell at 8:00 a.m.? This is insane! Maybe the landlord, did we miss the rent or something?"

I hopped out of bed, ran downstairs, and answered the door in just board shorts to see what was going on. Three 50-somethings were staring back at me. The man in front says, "Hello, we brought breakfast. Have you eaten yet?"

"I think you've got the wrong house. We don't know each other," I insisted.

"Aren't you part of Sourcebank.com?" the man asked, genuinely concerned if he'd rung the wrong door at this point.

"Umm, well, yeah."

"Hello, Neil, how are you?" My roommate Sameer comes bounding down the stairs in slacks and a button-up shirt. I'd never seen this shirt before. Apparently he'd forgotten to mention to me that this was happening. I should probably go find a shirt.

Several months before, Sameer, Sean, Josh, and I had created a specialized search engine for programmers. The idea was to organize the web's assets that were valuable to just programmers in one convenient location and make it easy to access and use. We had opted to try this out instead of a summer internship and had managed to pull it off, for the most part. We were generating some meager advertising revenue and figured with our last year of school coming up, we'd try to sell it off or run it ourselves.

In talking with a large search engine company that decided to pass on acquiring our little business, Sameer had been introduced to two angel investors, and they had brought Neil to talk to us about our business plan.

Neil was very direct. "This last sentence in your business plan, is this real? Can you really use all of the same tools you built for spidering, indexing, classifying, summarizing, and searching the web to do other things? Recipes, baseball cards, stamp collecting, etc.?"

Sameer had inserted that sentence to help people understand how four college kids could have put the whole site together in just three months. It wasn't because we were sorting it all manually. It was because we'd built software tools to do it all automatically. Only, the trick with our tools was that they were not completely handcrafted instructions to the computer. They were much more general and could be retooled to apply to any major subject of interest. Sameer tried to clarify that this was not automatic. "Well, we want to be clear, there is still a lot of work involved to retool them and it would be better if we had some more time to polish them up a bit for some new topic area we apply it to, but basically, yes."

Again Neil was direct, to the point, and did not mince any words. "Great, then the rest of this business plan, all of it except for that sentence, is a complete waste of time. The good news is that you know that now and we have time to fix it."

We? What was this guy talking about?

Next, Neil gave us his pitch about why selling Sourcebank.com was selling our future short. We had so much opportunity ahead of us in building tools that could help the next Amazon.com to sell books, the next Recipes.com, the next travel site, you name it! The Internet was starting to coalesce around destination sites that pulled everything together into the one authority people went to find stuff about each subject. Everyone was starting a new company to get their piece of the Internet Frontier, and we had tools that could help them do it.

This old man in a baseball cap told us we had to start a new company together, to provide services to help any new "portal" aggregate and index the web's content related to their area of the market.

It was around 9:30 a.m. when Neil was done talking, and he said, "What do you guys say, can I send you some paperwork to get this thing started?"

I was thoroughly confused. "What do you mean, to actually incorporate, go get an office, and start this company?"

Neil replied casually, "Of course, I'll do all the logistical horseshit, you don't need to worry about that." Then he realized he should turn up the volume a little to drive the point home. "We will have a real office, working phones, Internet, computers, whiteboards, office furniture, everything in two months. I will find us a marketing person and a salesperson. We'll start hiring more engineers soon after we get set up. Your job is to write the code. I'll take care of the rest."

Totally blown away, I replied quite genuinely, "Wow! Umm, well, I guess we'll think about it and get back to you?" We were overwhelmed with the possibilities, let alone the idea that we were going to walk away from a few hundred thousand dollars in quick money that another company had recently offered to pay for our company.

Author's note: The so-called offer was more of an expression of interest rather than a binding letter of intent but nonetheless, it is true that they could have made a couple bucks pretty quick. Their site, Sourcebank.com, was unique. There was clearly a deal on the table. Let's face it, these were way fucking smart kids.

Neil's expression was pure confusion. "What is there to think about?"

At this point I was starting to get a little nervous at the speed of the whole proceeding so I tried to communicate our concerns in a way that would make it clear that we weren't totally sold on the idea yet. "Well, there are several things. To start with, who the hell are you anyway?!? All we know is that you showed up at our door with some donuts."

Neil paused, looked at the other three guys, then back at me and smiled. "You've raised a fair point. Do some checking about me around town. I'm happy to offer some references. Here is my card if you have any further questions, and I will not call you unless you call me first. However, even if you decide to pass I would appreciate a courtesy phone call, just to let me know."

With that, the next four years would be a complete blur.

HIRING

We knew we needed some help from people who were older than us. We didn't have any kind of chip on our shoulders against the establishment, or any kind of belief that we knew what we were doing better than people our fathers' ages.

One of the most interesting things about starting a software company at the age of 21 is that we had to interview people who were definitely older and supposed to be more experienced than we were.

The first several times we interviewed someone in their mid-40s for what would now be called a Senior Database Architect was just tough. There were lots of weird social moments where we'd ask critical questions about their job history or their work on a project, and you could just tell that it was not a natural act for them to be critiqued by people half their age. As you repeat this process you learn some tricks to make the process go more smoothly. One technique is to keep the pace very quick and not dwell on anything for too long. The other is to focus on problems, not on historical projects. Finally, it became clear after a while that good senior people were generally more secure about being questioned by younger people because they had the goods to answer the questions we fired at them.

TECHNOLOGY

We started Mohomine building out a suite of technologies to help aggregate and utilize web text better. This meant a customizable web spider for getting pages from the web about specific topics, a customizable search engine for providing search across these pages, a very accurate Support Vector Machine (SVM) text classifier for sorting these pages, several Markov Model-based information extraction technologies in order to extract information from the pages, a summary snippet generator, and a web page clustering program to group pages together automatically without human intervention.

Technologically, we were pretty much up against Whizbang! Labs. They were the preeminent academics from around the world gathered together to apply information retrieval to real problems. They had created a very impressive site called Flipdog, which used their technology to automatically aggregate job postings so people could search for jobs available on the Internet in one place.

The primary problem with this of course was the business model. You can't charge people who don't have a job very much money. On the other hand, if companies are desperately trying to hire, they are happy to pay you money to improve or speed up their process. Therefore, inspired by this, we created a résumé extraction product. It became the preeminent résumé extraction software in the industry for several years until we sold it.

Author's note: It was this résumé application that we licensed to PeopleSoft that accounted for our first $1 million account.

TOUGH TIMES

To me, one of the most fascinating things about the Mohomine experience is that it was a constant struggle. Only in retrospect do I really appreciate how lucky we were to get that group of people together and to maintain the will to keep fighting.

Rule #67: The ultimate measure of a man is not where he stands in moments of comfort and convenience, but where he stands at times of challenge and controversy. —Martin Luther King Jr.

When things got difficult, not just for our company but our entire industry, the response from our team was pretty overwhelming. We had people with families and new babies taking salary cuts for indeterminate number of months while we tried desperately to raise the next round of money.

There were people working for days without rest to help get products out the door or address customer needs to help close deals. Others were on the road or on the phone constantly trying to drum up money, even $25,000 at a time—anything to weather the storm.

The first person you fire shouldn't be a friend of yours.

When you're growing a company from scratch, you reach out to everyone you know to come help you out. As college students, we recruited friends from high school and college. When you're pitching people to come join your new company that they've never heard of, it's a real task. You have to really be convincing that this is worth giving up a job at some real company to go change the world. You mean every word of it of course, but you can't half-ass the delivery or it just doesn't sound compelling enough.

Mohomine was no different. We recruited some great people we had classes with or even grew up with. Unfortunately, after doubling a few times in size, the texture and shape of the company changed. A few friends couldn't make the transition, and this was compounded even further by the huge economic downturn. We had to make some tough decisions, and some of our friends we rallied so hard to recruit were going to have to leave. Delivering this message and dealing with the aftermath is one of those things that you never forget.

Author's note: Sameer worked at Kofax for six years and is now at Google. Chris worked for a year at Kofax, left, and started his own company. He is now at Google. Sean is in a new software deal—with me.

CHAPTER 29

LATRODECTUS THERIDIIDAE

(A.K.A. THE BLACK WIDOW)

Rule #189: If the water is polluted, sometimes it is just easier to blow up the dam and start over.

There was a company in San Diego called Graviton. They had raised $40 million plus and were making very cool, very small mesh network sensors. The CEO spent like a drunken sailor, they couldn't find a big enough market, and the stuff didn't work quite right. Thus, in keeping with the immutable laws of interplanetary finance (those are the ones that speak of revenue, cost, margin, market, product design, customer acceptance, and burn rate), coupled with management disarray, anger, and litigation, the company imploded, quietly went broke, and closed.

However, there was one small issue. You see, one of Graviton's investors was In-Q-Tel. You remember them, the venture arm of the CIA? And those fellows in Langley, Virginia, wanted what they had bargained for, and they wanted it when they wanted it and where the hell was it, and "I don't give a damn if they went broke, we gave them money and we want the product we bargained for, so goddamnit, find it, fix it, and ship it."

We had just sold Mohomine to Kofax, and the government and the investors were happy. I had put my feet up for about two weeks when Gilman Louie, CEO of In-Q-Tel, called.

Rule #31: No good deed goes unpunished.

"Can you step in and fix a bit of a mess? You did such a good job running the last company into the ground, would you like to try again?"

How can you say no to an invitation like that?

My job was to take a small team from Graviton that was specifically working on the CIA project and lead them to the completion of the product. This proved to be extremely difficult, primarily because I made the classic mistake. I thought I could change the DNA of an inherited team, rather than build a new team from scratch. This was a major miscalculation.

Rule #259: The only thing a CEO should inherit is his or her mother's good silverware. Everything else—dishes, glasses, and placemats—buy new.

The project team that was working on the sensor network for the CIA was led by a very difficult woman who had somehow developed a Svengali hold on the existing team of 10 people who were in the aggregate somewhere north of difficult and 20 degrees east of dysfunctional. They had all been together at Graviton, and when I showed up as the new CEO of this new little spinout company, Soflinx, the only person who had worked with me before was Nicole. I had no friends on Day One.

And one might well argue that 18 months later, when we sold the new company, I also had no friends.

And thus began 18 months of brutal, depressing, and thankless effort at Soflinx, the worldwide leader in wireless mesh network sensors (or at least this is what the PR flack wrote when they launched the company).

The leader of this pack was a very smart, pathologically devious, blonde, attractive, incorrigible, and flirtatious woman engineer. The other nine geniuses treated her like the Queen Bee; they treated me as if I were the Orkin Man, pest control agent extraordinaire. She would flip her blond locks and her too-low-cut blouse, and the drones would salivate and line up attentively at their cubicles waiting for a drop of honey.

If I suggested that she needed to do something, the drones would rally around her and explain to me that I was an idiot. If I took her to task and set deliverables, the drones would buzz around, create havoc, and retreat to the hive, incommunicado.

I was dramatically inadequate in creating a new corporate culture. The same delays and disagreements that had plagued them at Graviton carried over to the new company. We had a contract to deliver something to the CIA, and we were woefully late and we weren't even sure it would work.

Rule #277: There is no such thing as a small mess. When asked to clean up a small mess, the first thing you should do is clean the whole house.

In retrospect, I should have removed 75 percent of the old team. But foolishly, I believed in my unlimited capacity to effect change and create a positive culture for Rational Man Behavior. I was wrong. It was a basic lesson, and I had forgotten it. And I will never, ever forget it again.

Rule #159: Never bet against the macro. If a hurricane is blowing, don't hang out the wash and expect it to dry.

There was only one thrilling moment in this adventure. I got to go back to Langley, during the installation and visit CIA Headquarters, the Agency, the real deal. You walk inside the building, past the huge logo on the floor, with the words "Central Intelligence Agency" in a semi-circle above the American Bald Eagle. If you don't get a tingle, then you are probably close to dead.

I got the tour. I got to see the secret museum in the basement where the history of spy versus spy is shown in glass cases. All the secret stuff you read about like cigarette lighters that were really cameras and pens that were really guns, James Bond is alive and well in Langley, Virginia.

And I must confess that I was moved. Even got a bit teary-eyed. When you see the history of the bad things and the bad people that have tried to hurt America, it does remind you that freedom is not free and patriotism is not cheap.

I was a child of the '60s and the Vietnam War (although I served in the Army Reserves) so I was never a big believer in government as an institution—but I did care deeply about finishing this job. I hated being at this little company and were it not for my own personal, maybe confused and certainly inflated, sense of patriotism, I would have resigned.

Rule #295: "You see, we're on a mission from God." —Elwood Blues, *The Blues Brothers*

In the end, the secret, cool stuff finally did get installed, it actually did work, and the Agency still uses it. The job was complete.

But we were a wounded company that could not survive. The boys at the Agency wanted the technology in the hands of a big, strong company, not a tiny start-up that was about to implode. Time to sell.

And once again, my job was to bundle this dog up and find a new owner; some unsuspecting, but trusting Fortune 500 company that could take the technology and expand it to more markets, as well as support the installation at the Agency.

While we were finishing the project for the CIA, we had received a proposal to install the technology around the perimeter of the main stadium at the Greek Olympics. At this time I got another of the many lessons I have so frequently received on the subject of graft, corruption, and self-dealing. The magnitude of the duplicity, crookery, and connivery was beyond my skill set. We danced with Athens for five months but in the end there was no deal.

"Beware of Greeks bearing gifts" needed to be rewritten as simply "Beware of Greeks."

And then we got a break.

I would suggest to you, dear reader, that I have been overly fortunate over too many years in pulling rabbits from hats. I have used my allotted nine lives, more than three times over. For certain, I am living on borrowed time, and there was clearly a shit storm waiting to happen to me. Which in fact is exactly what happened with the next company. But that tale will have to wait for the next book. My fury is still too palpable.

But for Soflinx, it was time for one last top hat and one last rabbit.

Rule #76: Magic is conjuring tricks and illusions that make apparently impossible things seem to happen, usually performed as entertainment unless the entire financial well-being of the company depends on it, in which case there is nothing funny about sawing a lady in half, which if not done carefully, can result in great loss of blood and bankrupt the company.

There was a large contract being let to protect a bunch of bridges in New York City with a massive wireless sensor network. Our technology would be perfect. There were three companies bidding, and one was Lockheed Martin. Once again, we had the best technology. And once again we started the dance.

I learned to dance at cotillion. Growing up in St. Louis in the '50s, young men and women of a certain breeding were required to learn how to dance. It was organized and promoted by the National League of Junior Cotillions. Their mission statement was and is "Committed to standards of excellence in the development of teaching character and social education of today's youth." I will keep my opinion on this to myself.

There were monthly dances where we were encouraged to learn etiquette, manners, dance steps (no making it up as you go along), proper address, and above all else, we were strongly discouraged from trying to touch our partner's breasts during the slow dances. Which was the only reason to go to this thing anyway.

I ended up being a reasonably good dancer (at least that is what my wife thinks) but it was awkward, uncomfortable, and only served to reinforce class and social distinctions that were vestiges of a dying period, soon to be relegated to only a minority of the very rich. St. Louis society had debutantes who came out. I never knew anyone who "came out," except maybe from the closet.

Lockheed Martin needed the technology in order to complete their bid on the job. As part of their submission, they had to demonstrate that they had technology capable of doing the work.

They offered to license the technology. I rejected that idea. I told them that if they wanted the stuff, they would have to buy the company.

This was a bit high-handed to say the least, and they were more than nonplussed at our insistence. It was the equivalent of a young lady saying she won't sleep with you until she is married, and your retort is that you won't marry her until you sleep with her.

In matters of technology for a $46 billion company, let it suffice that abstinence did not make the heart grow fonder. They were not amused. But the deadline for the bid was approaching.

Allow me to describe the fine points of the Vienna waltz.

First call.

"You pick a number, no, too low, OK, pick again, still too low. My turn to pick, oh too high, well then, pick your nose."

Next call.

"I know you are a big company. That's why we are talking to you—because you have the money. I'm sympathetic. Of course I know you can't turn the Queen Mary around in a day, but we need to close soon."

Next call.

"OK, so maybe I was a bit rash. Let's try again. All right, now that number has some possibilities. You are definitely getting very warm, but you mentioned that you wanted to review 293 things during due diligence. I see, well, that will take about five months, and oh, isn't the bid due in 17 days?"

They closed in 15 days, and they won the bid.

I love to dance. I was born to dance. Unfortunately, Broadway is not crying out for short, Jewish dancers.

Lockheed kept four members of the team. The rest disbanded and went who knows where. The pretty lady disappeared. The agency was happy. The technology was in secure hands. The bridges got their sensors, and our company closed.

About three months later I got a letter from Gilman thanking me for my effort at Soflinx on behalf of the Agency, and telling me that the government was grateful. Sounds corny but it meant a great deal to me.

I framed the letter, and even though I am still a bit uncomfortable when it comes to unbridled flag waving, my country right or wrong, mom and apple pie, when I hear "The Star Spangled Banner," I do get a bit teary. And, yes, I do believe in heroes.

CHAPTER 30

"IF I KNEW YOU WERE COMING, I WOULD HAVE BAKED A CAKE"

(THE COOKIE MONSTER)

I am fascinated by the concept of pattern recognition. I believe it is the single most important characteristic in entrepreneurial success. Pattern recognition is defined as "the act of taking in raw data and taking an action based on the category of the pattern."

But in order to execute and take advantage of pattern recognition, one needs to first acquire "10,000 chunks of knowledge." The man behind this concept was Dr. Jeffrey A. Timmons. Timmons was the one of the first who believed that entrepreneurship could be taught. He graduated from Harvard Business School in 1971 and in 1973 launched the first undergraduate major in new venture creation and entrepreneurship at Northeastern University. He went on to teach at Harvard and then, as the truly iconic entrepreneur that he was, he resigned a tenured chair at Harvard to start the entrepreneurship program at Babson College. Babson was rated #1 in entrepreneurship for 12 straight years under Timmons, and he was one of the top professors on the subject in the country. Read his book, *New Venture Creation*.

I had the opportunity to study with him for one week at Babson as part of a program to learn how to teach entrepreneurship. The program was interesting; he was amazing. He died in June 2008—a tremendous loss to the field of entrepreneurship.

So you have to give credit where credit is due. While much has been written about pattern recognition, Timmons did the hard work of explaining how to get the data so you can see the pattern. You need both pieces of the puzzle. Today data mining is a billion dollar business with all the major companies sending cookies, breaking cookies, eating cookies, and trying to find and make sense of your pattern.

But at the human, individual, entrepreneur level, the issue of the "10,000" is really just a nice way of saying you need to get your brains beat in a few dozen times so you can get some experience. Experience is not cheap. If it were, it wouldn't be valuable.

Rule #165: The trick is to figure out who is the guy with the gloves on, who is the referee, and who is the round card girl in the push-up bra—before you get knocked flat on your ass. Then, when the bell rings for the next round, you are there for him, baby (with a baseball bat!).

The power of pattern recognition in the software industry is wide spread and well known. It is why Larry Ellison is very rich. He makes it easy to put things in columns and rows that let you "crunch" the data, and it is the crunching of the data that drives 90 percent of Wall Street trading. It is pattern recognition that has fueled the rise of the "quant" boys. And their power is the ability to assimilate 10,000 chunks of knowledge in a second and act on it in another microsecond.

But for us mere mortals, getting experience that is actionable takes time and is hard work. It involves failure. Nobody bats .1000. Call it a feedback loop or call it falling off your bike, acquiring chunks of knowledge is a lifetime pursuit.

Rule #199: If it were easy, everyone would do it.

I've always been fascinated by the chess masters. In 1972, the "Match of the Century" between Bobby Fischer and Boris Spassky captivated the world and served as the symbolic political confrontation between the two superpowers during the Cold War.

In 1989, the match between reigning world chess champion Garry Kasparov and IBM's Deep Blue Thought supercomputer captivated the world again. The computer was capable of analyzing 200 million positions per second. IBM won 4-2.

So what is it? As an entrepreneur, how do you begin to see the patterns in your daily life and having seen them, how you integrate them and act on the knowledge?

An easy answer is that skill comes with age. I don't think so. Look at Gates, Jobs, Brin, Zuckerberg. Their successes came early in their lives in terms of chronological age. They saw connections that others didn't.

But by the same token, fewer than 10 CEOs of Fortune 500 companies are under the age of 35. Michael Dell became the youngest CEO of a Fortune 500 company at the age of 27. The average age of a Fortune 500 CEO is 56. So maybe gray counts for something.

But I suspect the underlying dirty little secret is that pattern recognition favors the entrepreneur more than the manager. Pattern recognition is the DNA of the start-up. It is the assessing and then the assembling that lead to the synthesis of an idea and then the willingness to begin to execute.

Rule #43: Your ability to acquire valuable experience is dramatically enhanced and sharpened by the fact that you have to deal with the direct consequences of your own decision making.

There is nothing like being personally responsible for the fuckups. When you have your own money in the game, you really do count the paper clips, and with a 50X magnifying glass, you search for the revenue opportunities.

It is said that it is always nice to learn on someone else's nickel. Maybe, but when it's your nickel, you tend to learn a little faster.

My son called recently and asked, "During your career, did you ever wonder what you would do if the venture or project failed?"

I found the question fascinating. As I thought about it, I wanted to confess to him that of course I was afraid. When you have almost all of your chips in the center of the table, it would be insane not to, at least for a moment, wonder what you are going to do when the other guy shows up with pocket aces.

Rule #47: You cannot let the fear paralyze you.

I told my son that the trick to overcoming paralysis is to learn to have a 360-degree view of yourself. I have learned how to do this after 35 years of psychoanalysis. I can talk to all the people in the room, each of which is a fraction of the whole me, and in so doing, manage, assess, react to, quantify, and deal with the fear.

I do not want you to think I am a Zen nut case. This is a common technique. It is simply the ability (and I believe the requirement) to be able to stand apart, to have an interior dialogue with the various participants at the table—all of whom are in some way yourself. In effect, you are looking in at a hall of mirrors, not unlike the scene in *Lady from Shanghai* by Orson Welles.

In any scenario, there is always the observer. Your skill in developing pattern recognition will be enhanced if you can create within yourself an observer who is the Absolutely Rational Man. Then, allow the various dialogues to proceed, and in my experience, more often than not, clarity shows up brightly. The concept of an interior monologue is a well-known technique. I think a constant interior dialogue leads to much clearer pattern recognition.

Rule #149: It is the continual refinement and replaying of the history of the past moments that lead to the current "Aha!" moment of either inspiration or recognition. And in that moment, it becomes obvious what the proper next step should be.

If you are climbing a big mountain such as Everest or K-2, you are certainly keenly aware that things could turn out badly. You can slip, fall, and die. That can also happen right in your little cubicle.

I told my son that I have always lived with the demons of failure. I am haunted in that regard. But I also told him that I have been very lucky, much more so than would seem statistically normal.

I am always struck by this dichotomy. Some of the most fortunate people do not really understand how lucky they have been. My view is a simple one. I have been blessed; I know it and am grateful.

Rule #53: You can never go wrong being grateful.

It seems that I have been fortunate to find the clue, the last piece of the puzzle, so many times—and always just in the nick of time like the *Perils of Pauline*, right before the saw cuts her in half or the train runs her over or the barrel goes over the falls. I have way overstayed my welcome when it comes to good fortune. I have been very lucky. Very, very lucky.

But then my son points out that it can't be just luck because it has happened too many times. The odds are irrational, inconsistent, out of the standard deviation by at least two orders of magnitude. So if it is not luck, what is it?

How many times can something or someone materialize just as you need it? In other words, can one's human passion, effort, and determination bend the statistical laws of the universe and bring you triumph—not only against all odds but also in spite of all odds?

It doesn't seem rational. And this book tries hard to trumpet the cause for Rational Man Behavior.

Now the hard question is this: Can you count on it, can you play for it, can you assume that like the trapeze artist who lets go and does the somersault before the other person is there ready to catch him, anticipating that he will get there by the time you get to where you are supposed to be caught, that in fact the other person, having left at a later time, ends up there just in time is there for you, baby, right then and there and catches you in his grip and you are alive and well and do not fall to the floor?

Can you anticipate that like some James Bond movie, just as the bomb is about to blow up, the wire will get cut or the computer code will freeze the numbers and the world will be saved and you along with it?

Is that part of being an entrepreneur?

It's outrageously arrogant to even consider it and yet, maybe that is one small key to the puzzle. I am not sure. Maybe it is exactly the assumption that whoever/whatever needs to be there for you, baby, will actually be there for you, baby, when you arrive at the spot in the time that you need it.

Rule #409: You have to release the trapeze and do the somersault before you see the hands of your partner. If you wait to see him and then start your somersault you will fail—and fall.

Rule #409 is known as the leap of faith. Take it.

Everyone has images and icons that inform and transform behavior. In my case, I have created an avatar that takes its form as John Elway or Joe Montana. I want to come into the game with the ball on my own

20 with a minute and 29 seconds left to play. I believe I will drive down to the opponent's 12-yard line and then on a simple pass play into the corner, both feet in bounds, with three seconds on the clock, done deal. I love it.

I am going to apologize to all right now. I recognize that this is an utter and complete fantasy. First of all, I am 5'7", 158 pounds, and I cannot throw a football 15 yards. But in my mind's eye, it is another story.

The image of Montana and Elway, who have done this countless times, informs how I think of entrepreneurship. A quarterback's greatest skill is pattern recognition. He "reads" the defense.

And then psychology kicks in. The other side worries because it is Elway and, oh shit, he is going to do this to us again. And Elway has the benefit of the other side already thinking that about his reputation, and so he gets the added element. Imagine negotiating against Donald Trump, Michael Bloomberg, Warren Buffet, Mike Milken, Bill Gates, etc. There is history, and there is the element of unpredictability. Adding a touch of "wild man" to the mix gives you an edge if it is authentic, if there is a legitimate history of similar behavior.

But even with the edge, even with the reputation, I posit that the principal actor, the one seeking the successful outcome in the drama, the one who is being counted on to deliver the results, still has the fear of failure. You cannot be great if you are not grounded at some level in basic fear. Not the fear of can I succeed in this event but WILL I succeed? No matter the level of confidence, lurking in the wings is a rational voice that says, maybe this time I am going to come up short.

This mélange, this stew of confidence, arrogance, and luck often come together in the entrepreneurial drama. It is why you can teach the principles but you cannot teach someone to be an entrepreneur. There are simply too many ingredients in the recipe.

Let's take a peek at George Steinbrenner's history. In 1971, he tried to buy the Cleveland Indians and after extensive negotiations, Vernon Stouffer, the owner who was the frozen food king, turned him down. He felt that George was not paying enough. The offered price was $8 million. The asking was $9 million.

A year later, together with some friends, Steinbrenner paid CBS $10 million for the New York Yankees. Steinbrenner wanted a baseball team, and the truth is he got lucky that he didn't get the one he first wanted. Not smart, just lucky.

Fay Vincent, the former commissioner of Major League Baseball, attributes the following quote to John McMullen, the former owner of the Houston Astros:

"Fay, you only have to make one good deal in your lifetime to be successful."

I think that is a powerful sentence. We have all seen the results of that sentence. If you probe the story behind a rich guy, you often find that he bought an apartment building 20 years ago and then by chance they built the City Hall right next to it or he had one good idea (a gizmo or a food product or a technology) and he sold it at the right time—and he never did another.

The entrepreneur has a slightly different mindset. He needs to go up to the plate frequently. His is not a one-swing effort. No one wants to be a one-trick pony. You need to prove that it wasn't a fluke.

Steinbrenner caught the perfect wave at the perfect time. His story reminds us of the need for the fortuitous amalgam of time, history, and the characters acting on that stage at that moment. All must coalesce in order to achieve the larger-than-life outcomes.

Rule #201: Never ever underestimate the power of timing and good fortune.

So here is the final question: Can you get good enough at pattern recognition so that you can influence luck and propitious timing? Can you bend reality and turn it into your fantasies?

I think you can but I am not sure I can explain exactly how. I am a man of pragmatic beliefs, I embrace Rational Man Behavior, I am an empiricist. But at the same time I believe in magic and unexplained phenomena. I accept that I cannot know exactly how things come to pass. I believe in revelations as much as I do in solutions.

I have always loved the quantum mechanics concept behind the Heisenberg Uncertainty Principle. It states that precise inequalities, like position and momentum, cannot simultaneously be known to an arbitrary precision. In other words, the more you know about the position of a particle, the less you can know about its velocity. You can't know both position and speed with the same degree of exactitude.

Rule #315: You can know how fast you are going headed over the cliff, but you can't know exactly where the edge is.

CONCLUSION

(THERE IS NO CONCLUSION. THE ENTREPRENEUR IS NEVER DONE)

How can you not stand up and cheer for Sidney Harman who, at 92 years old, bought *Newsweek*? I love that story. His wife is 65. He has a billion dollars, and he bought a money-losing magazine in the midst of a digital revolution with the idea of turning it back into something great that makes money. He's 92 so he's not planning on it taking 15 years to get to break-even.

There are another 1,000 stories that elevate the human spirit. Medicine, technology, green tech, energy, etc. The list is enormous if not endless.

I'm a storyteller, and there's a lot of material. What no one can be sure of is how much time is left on the clock. There are no guarantees.

Rule #101: Entrepreneurs have an abiding sense of urgency because they know that what they regret most is not the things they did do, but the things they didn't do.

Dear reader: Entrepreneurship is a mantle to be worn with grace, humility, and a deep appreciation of the joys and the perils that it provides. I hope that some of these stories will give you a few touchstones to consider as you navigate your own road.

Enjoy the trip, and along the way, may each of you find the compatible soul who is truly there for you, baby.

APPENDIX: THE BABY RULES

RULE #	THE RULE	LOCATION
1	Return every email and every phone call.	Chapter 1, 5, 12
2	Networking is a profession. Become a professional at it.	Chapter 3, 12
3	You must go to every meeting and every event; in particular, the ones you know for sure will be a total waste of time.	Chapter 3
5	The wheel is always spinning.	Chapter 6
6	The heart often yearns for things that money cannot buy.	Chapter 11
9	Do not ever let a bank act as trustee for your heirs and assignees.	Chapter 6
11	Persuaders give reasons. Negotiators give concessions.	Chapter 9
18	Rules are not made to be broken.	Chapter 4
19	Entrepreneurs do not do it for fame or fortune—they do it for revenge	Chapter 10, 12
23	Keeping your problems to yourself ensures that no one else can help you. If you don't give out your address, how can anyone find your house?	Chapter 12
28	Dilution is relatively meaningless.	Chapter 8
29	It never hurts to pitch one down the middle early with a little ego balm on it.	Chapter 3

RULE #	THE RULE	LOCATION
31	No good deed goes unpunished.	Chapter 2, 29
32	The screwing that you're getting may not be worth the screwing you're getting.	Chapter 3
38	No matter what, you should always be polite.	Chapter 24
39	You can either pick the terms or the price, but you can't pick both.	Chapter 2
40	Things are never what they seem, nor are the people involved with those things.	Chapter 3
41	Why take a good customer and turn him into a suspicious, disbelieving, untrusting consumer who no longer believes in you, your product or your supposed customer service—just because you can.	Chapter 21
42	Find out who the true decision maker is and deal with him/her.	Chapter 27
43	Your ability to acquire valuable experience is dramatically enhanced and sharpened by the fact that you have to deal with the direct consequences of your own decision making.	Chapter 30
44	Don't spend investor money if there is no hope. They will remember the kindness in the future.	Chapter 5
47	You cannot let the fear paralyze you.	Chapter 30
48	One big customer can also bury a company.	Chapter 12
53	You can never go wrong being grateful. When you get to heaven and at the gate, you are asked by God whether he should rule on your life with justice or mercy—no contest, you have to pick mercy.	Chapter 30
55	One good deed deserves another. So, what have you done for me lately?	Chapter 13
56	Be willing to make trade-offs	Chapter 11
57	There is always a competitor. Followers of the Sun Tzu understand this axiom well. Make your competitor your ally	Chapter 13
59	Negotiating is like riding a bike—everyone can do it at some level. And then there is Lance Armstrong.	Chapter 9
65	The rats are running the renewal business	Chapter 21

RULE #	THE RULE	LOCATION
66	"Make me an offer" is a reasonable response to almost everything. (Not including when your wife asks you to take out the trash.)	Chapter 9
67	The ultimate measure of a man is not where he stands in moments of comfort and convenience, but where he stands at times of challenge and controversy.—Martin Luther King, Jr.	Chapter 28
71	Publicity is powerful—especially if they spell your name correctly.	Chapter 12
72	When a goose walks in the door, don't be so fast to close it. You won't know if it is golden, until you hear him quack.	Chapter 24
73	The desire to change can only come after an awareness of the need for change.	Chapter 24
74	The power and desire for financial innovation will always trump rules designed to mandate fairness, transparency and equity.	Chapter 2
75	You can't—until you can.	Chapter 12
77	No one likes to be replaced.	Chapter 13
76	Magic is conjuring tricks and illusions that make apparently impossible things seem to happen, usually performed as entertainment—unless the entire financial well-being of the company depends on it, in which case there is nothing funny about sawing a lady in half, which if not done carefully, can result in great loss of blood and bankrupt the company.	Chapter 29
78	If you have them by the balls, their hearts and minds will follow—this rule is credited to General William Westmoreland and his assessment of the likelihood of our success in Vietnam.	Chapter 3
79	The only thing worse than not getting what you want is getting what you want and not knowing it.	Chapter 9
81	Find the subtext. Things are never quite what they seem to be.	Chapter 13
82	A can opener beats using your teeth every time.	Chapter 4
83	If you don't know how deep the water is, diving head first is simply the triumph of terror over caution.	Chapter 25

RULE #	THE RULE	LOCATION
84	Sucking up to the king works best when you can throw someone else under the bus to enhance your own position	Chapter 3
85	Don't be greedy.	Chapter 7
87	When holding pocket aces, do not play your cards as if they were off-suited 3 and 8.	Chapter 17
88	When you hear those magic words, "We can do that deal" bend over and grab your ankles. The corollary, "Done deal" requires a similar position.	Chapter 2
89	The lament is never solely about money	Chapter 11
90	When the standard solution doesn't work, create a new solution.	Chapter 26
91	This is what is known as good news and bad news. The good news: Microsoft is calling. The bad news: Microsoft is calling. And thus began our "partnership" with Bill and the boys from Red- mond. It turned out they didn't want to crush us; they wanted to help us (to help them).	Chapter 13
92	If you are the richest guy at the table, find another table.	Chapter 7
93	Do not hide the truth from your people.	Chapter 13
94	Listen carefully—good ideas may be spoken softly	Chapter 13
95	Don't forget. Short term memory loss or revisionist history does not cut it.	Chapter 3
96	Don't think just because you know what to do that the other guy will reach the same conclusion. Refer back to Kahneman on rational man behavior and acting in one's own perceived best self interest.	Chapter 6
97	One size does not fit all, even in condoms. Measure the other side carefully. It matters.	Chapter 9
98	The only business more rotten than the used car business is the movie business.	Chapter 10
99	Waiting is more painful than a proctology exam—the first person to talk loses.	Chapter 3

RULE #	THE RULE	LOCATION
100	If you are running down a road and you look back and there is no one following you—there are two and only two possibilities—one, you are way the fuck ahead—two, you are on the wrong road.	Chapter 4
101	Entrepreneurs have an abiding sense of urgency, because they know that what they regret most is not the things they did do, but the things they didn't do.	Conclusion
102	Don't offer evil, rapacious, stupid terms to your angel investors—even if you can get away with it. That kind of deal structure will come back to haunt you.	Chapter 8
104	A lot of people talk about the next level. Talk is cheap. It requires massive commitment and a tall ladder. There are no elevators.	Chapter 24
107	Know your customer. I was already selling to the pushers; I just needed a bigger stash.	Chapter 2
108	Never eat grapefruit at a breakfast meeting.	Chapter 10
109	Never let the truth get in the way of a good story.	Preface, Chapter 3, 12
110	Do not pick up the phone and call them. Do not pick up the phone and call them. Do not pick up the phone and call them.	Chapter 25
111	Whenever possible hire the very best—and pay the freight.	Chapter 27
113	There is a reason that the mafia is Italian. The only rolling over that occurred in this deal was when his truck rolled over my leg and broke my kneecap.	Chapter 4
119	"I made all my money by selling too soon."—J. Pierpont Morgan	Chapter 3
120	You can't go broke taking a profit.	Chapter 3
121	How ya gonna keep 'em down on the farm after they've seen Paree.	Chapter 11
122	It is always more fun to date than it is to get married.	Chapter 3
127	Get a new pair of glasses.	Chapter 7
129	When marrying, if you have a choice, pick brains over money.	Chapter 11

RULE #	THE RULE	LOCATION
131	Your most important asset is human capital.	Chapter 11
132	If there are four founders, it doesn't mean that the equity should necessarily be split equally, 25% each. Life isn't fair.	Chapter 25
133	"What will happen if we go broke" is the one question you can never really answer well. Everybody's tolerance for risk, pain, disappointment, loss and potentially having to start over is different. Whatever your answer, you must never lie to your potential employee. Never.	Chapter 27
134	The reason that Al Pacino (you may substitute any of the 25 other names here) is a great actor is because you believe he is the character.	Chapter 17
135	It is all about acting and performance. Make the audience believe the character. Be the character.	Chapter 27
138	If it is such a good deal, why are you calling me?	Chapter 2
139	If you borrow $5000 and don't pay it back the bank will come after you—they are the lender and you are the borrower, and you promised you would pay them back the money. They will track you to the darkest cave in Afghanistan. If you borrow $100M, and can't pay it back, the bank might come after you—but at that point, they are not really your lender anymore, THEY ARE YOUR PARTNER	Chapter 3
144	You made your bed, now you have to lie in it—unless the sheets are dirty.	Chapter 3
149	Do not get on the plane unless you are prepared to deliver a great performance.	Chapter 17
150	It is the continual refinement and replaying of the history of the past moments that lead to the current "aha" moment of either inspiration or recognition. And it that moment, it becomes obvious what the proper next step should be.	Chapter 30
154	"Abandon hope, all ye who enter here."—Dante Alighieri	Chapter 27
159	Never be against the macro. If a hurricane is blowing, don't hang out the wash and expect it to dry.	Chapter 29
161	When traveling in darkness, bring a flashlight—and extra batteries. It could take longer than you think.	Introduction

RULE #	THE RULE	LOCATION
163	Your key people need to be accommodated. They are very hard to replace and frankly, you don't' want to.	Chapter 26
165	The trick is to figure out who is the guy with the gloves on, who is the referee, and who is the round card girl in the push-up bra—before you get knocked flat on your ass. Then, when the bell rings for the next round, you are there for him baby—with a baseball bat.	Chapter 30
167	They always get caught. That is why civilization works so well.	Chapter 16
177	If a deal is too good to be true, then look for the gray steak. There is always at least one in every box.	Chapter 15
179	Where you stand dramatically affects your point of view. Perspective and risk assessment are variables. It depends which end of the telescope you look through.	Chapter 25
182	If you want my assets, don't convince me that you will outperform the benchmark averages—convince me that you will take care of me—that you will love me—that I will be first among equals.	Chapter 19
183	The people who have the least money in the deal are usually the same people who have the strongest opinions about what they want you to do with your money.	Chapter 3
188	Do not bullshit a bullshitter.	Chapter 2
189	If the water is polluted, sometimes it is just easier to blow up the dam and start over.	Chapter 29
192	"What we have here is a failure to communicate." —Cool Hand Luke, 1967	Chapter 3
193	There are always forces at play that you know nothing about. Try to understand them before it is too late.	Chapter 11
194	No one is that good a skier!	Chapter 24
195	You can defer legal fees but you cannot avoid them	Chapter 6
198	No good deed goes unpunished.	Chapter 2

RULE #	THE RULE	LOCATION
199	The lessons of life are expensive and painful—they cannot be bought on the cheap. Do not demean them. Treasure them and cherish them and announce them—you will feel better afterwards and you will be able to look your kids in the eye.	Chapter 4
197	If it were easy, everyone would do it.	Chapter 30
200	After ten years you can take the hairshirt off your net worth statement. After all, even purgatory does not last for eternity.	Chapter 4
201	Never ever underestimate the power of timing and good fortune.	Chapter 30
202	The reason to sell something that doesn't exist is that deadlines can be liberating.	Chapter 12
204	More money is lost through neurotic behavior than through bad business decisions.	Chapter 6
205	Always be willing to renegotiate.	Chapter 7
206	When you have the upper hand with more perfect knowledge and you are negotiating with someone less skilled at the art of finance than you are, then it is incumbent, it is required, it is absolute that you must negotiate for him and actually make the deal better than he would have on his own.	Chapter 8
207	Chutzpah—it is like pornography. I can't define it, but I know it when I see it.	Chapter 17
208	Never, ever discount the power of good fortune.	Chapter 11
209	Who you know can be really important if you know who you know.	Chapter 25
212	When the government imposes stupid rules, take advantage of them.	Chapter 6
213	Never, ever discount the power of time and timing	Chapter 11
215	Time and timing.	Chapter 11
216	Objects in the mirror are closer than they appear.	Chapter 12
217	You don't know what you don't know.	Chapter 1,3

RULE #	THE RULE	LOCATION
218	Grand passion (and relentless pursuit) will take you further than good grades.	Chapter 4
219	All that riding will wear out a few pair of horseshoes. Find a good blacksmith	Chapter 4
220	Treat your superstars well, if not, they may leave and take your universe with them.	Chapter 16,17
221	If you can't find something nice to say about someone, don't say anything at all -- Ancient Proverb	Chapter 13
222	No limit poker subjects you to the principle of being table staked, which means the guy with the most money raises the pot until you have no more money to put in and you have to leave the tale. Not a good outcome.	Chapter 3
224	The question should not be how can we get more customers, it should be how can we get better customers	Chapter 19
225	Can you spell self-destructive?	Chapter 7
226	It's the going round and round that makes you crazy.	Chapter 25
227	Whenever possible, play to your strength.	Chapter 13
228	The best ideas often come from the factory floor. Make sure the floor has a direct elevator to management.	Chapter 13
229	The value of your company lies primarily in the work force.	Chapter 8
230	If it were easy, anybody could do it.	Chapter 13
231	"No" is just a speed bump on the road to yes.	Chapter 11, 18
232	"Nobody knows anything"—William Goldman,	Chapter 10
238	If you play tennis with yourself, you can never serve an ace	Chapter 7
240	I never forget.	Chapter 13
242	Nicole knows best.	Chapter 24

RULE #	THE RULE	LOCATION
243	Do you actually think your customer is stupid or do you just treat him that way?	Chapter 22
244	Clarity of thinking is improved when there is only one variable in play.	Chapter 3
245	All deals get made for more than one reason. Find the other one, that is the one that will drive the deal.	Chapter 7
246	When the woman in your life is smarter than you are, don't get confused by the male gene for pride and stupidity. First, ask—and if that doesn't work, then beg.	Chapter 11
248	When standing in line everybody lies a little. By the time you get to the pasta salad, everyone lies a lot.	Chapter 3
249	If you can't find a partner willing to get in the boat and go over the falls, then maybe the boat leaks. You didn't bring a patch kit?	Chapter 4
250	Look at the cover page before you hand me the book	Chapter 19
253	Silence is a powerful negotiating tool.	Chapter 9
255	If you think the service you provide is a commodity then you have diminished its worth and cannot properly value it.	Chapter 19
256	The customer is always right.	Chapter 12
257	Behind all the stated reasons is usually a real reason and a real motive.	Chapter 9
258	Nothing will prepare a CEO for working with engineering, genius, arrogant, difficult, uncommunicative, neurotic, brilliant people—nothing!!	Chapter 27
259	The only thing a CEO should inherit is your mother's good silverware. Everything else—dishes, glasses and placemats—buy it new.	Chapter 29
260	When someone very smart does something for you that seems dumb, remember to say, "thank you" . . . they are not stupid	Chapter 3
261	It's not rocket science, it's brain surgery.	Introduction
263	Collusion is just another word for joint venture.	Chapter 13
270	Read the fine print. Skimming is fine for Civilization 105, great books of the western world, but legal documents require a finer comb.	Chapter 6

RULE #	THE RULE	LOCATION
271	High risk insanity may cause damage to your marriage.	Chapter 7
272	Create something you can give away.	Chapter 27
273	Some deals are always in flux	Chapter 17
275	Whenever possible, get a great mentor. Get a great mentor.	Chapter 19
276	That is why they pay guys like Joe Torre and Phil Jackson a lot of money. Coaching is not the same as just watching the game from the bench.	Chapter 17
277	There is no such thing as a small mess. When asked to clean up a small mess, the first thing you should do is clean the whole house.	Chapter 29
278	That American Flag thing does kind of put a different spin on things.	Chapter 27
281	If no one else will jump in the pool, then look down first and see if there is any water in it before you launch off the high board doing a back flip with a 2 ½ twist.	Chapter 4
282	Rule 221 is utter and complete bullshit. If the guy is a fucking dummy, tell him that to his face.	Chapter 13
283	"Pressure is playing for ten dollars, when you don't have a dime in your pocket."—Lee Trevino	Chapter 3
284	Listen to the words, but more importantly, focus on the meaning behind them.	Chapter 18
285	Never stand on principle when a ladder is available.	Chapter 6
286	People in glass houses should not throw stones. Or they should have Lexan windows.	Chapter 15
288	The issue of fair negotiation is even more important when hiring employees.	Chapter 8
289	Hey, dude, talent rules. Follow the talent; do not force the talent to follow you. Example—Google has 67 corporate offices around the world including 21 in the United States.	Chapter 17
290	When in Rome, do not argue with the guy who manages the chariots.	Chapter 23
291	Beware of the word visionary. It often means someone who desperately needs Lasik surgery.	Chapter 3

RULE #	THE RULE	LOCATION
292	There is a fishhook in every deal, if you cannot find the fishhook, then do not take the bait.	Chapter 4
293	"We're putting the band back together." —Jake Blues	Chapter 6
294	It is important to know the difference between blind, dumb luck and actually thinking you know what the fuck you are doing.	Chapter 11
295	"You see, we're on a mission from God." —Elwood Blues	Chapter 29
296	So, what's in it for me?	Chapter 2
297	Fuck that fat lady singing—it is never over.	Chapter 3
298	Time and timing matter.	Chapter 7
299	Don't tell me about lemons and lemonade . . . just give me a Hendricks martini straight up.	Chapter 3
300	It never hurts to ask.	Chapter 6
302	More money is lost through neurotic behavior than through bad business decisions.	Chapter 6, 25
303	Behind every great fortune lies a great crime." —Honore de Balzac	Introduction, Chapter 2, 15
305	Know your opponent's style and adapt your game to his. You need lots of different shots—you can't just play big serve and volley.	Chapter 3
306	Bad decisions often come from places that are not easy to see until you pull back the covers and see whose horse head is in the bed.	Chapter 7
307	Always bet on the jockey. This rule is inviolate.	Chapter 25
308	Deal making can be a disease—get help soon than later.	Chapter 4
309	Never bullshit a bullshitter	Chapter 19
311	Sometimes you have the brass ring in your hand and you don't know it. When you look back and see it, you will wonder for a long time shy you didn't recognize it when it counted.	Chapter 25

RULE #	THE RULE	LOCATION
313	Do not believe your own bullshit.	Chapter 3
314	It doesn't matter what you pay for something when you buy it. It only matters what you sell it for later.	Chapter 13
315	You can know how fast you are going, headed over the cliff, but you can't know exactly where the fuck the edge of the cliff is.	Chapter 30
316	Time actually does slow down when you are waiting for it to run out.	Chapter 6
317	Do not ever underestimate the power of good weather.	Chapter 13
318	Because it is the right thing to do.	Chapter 7
319	Entrepreneurship is alive and well in Estonia	Chapter 23
321	Why is it so easy to see crazy, insane, stupid behavior in others and so hard to see it in ourselves.	Chapter 20
322	Make sure everyone on the boat has a chance to sit on the top deck in the sun.	Chapter 12
327	If you act illogically, stupidly and venally, your customers will eventually figure it out and you will be fucked.	Chapter 21
333	God occasionally gives you a chance to do a mitzvah or be a mensch. Never pass up any of these opportunities.	Chapter 7
336	When you do something really dumb, make sure you remember it so you don't do it again.	Chapter 4
337	When the Cheese Shop bill comes into my office, it is paid within 24 hours.	Chapter 18
339	Not knowing all the facts can prevent you from taking yourself out of the deal before you even get into it. Perfect knowledge leads to perfect paralysis.	Chapter 6
345	At the beginning of every adventure, one or two people will prove to be invaluable. They are seldom the people you think they will be.	Chapter 12
347	Your best friends are still the guys from high school.	Chapter 19

RULE #	THE RULE	LOCATION
362	You can't know what the other guy is going to say until you give him a chance to say it and you can't give him a chance to say it unless you ask and then shut up and wait.	Chapter 7
363	It never hurts to ask—as long as you ask politely and in a soft tone of voice.	Chapter 7
388	It is okay to draw a line in the sand, but be very careful about drawing one in concrete. Sand doesn't harden as quickly.	Chapter 27
390	Are you out of your fucking mind?	Chapter 7
391	If a studio executive said no to every picture that was brought to him to be made, he would have been right 82% of the time.	Chapter 10
392	The rich vs. king principle is a simple one. Do you want to be king and in total control of your territory? Or do you want to be rich?	Chapter 25
398	Motivations are different for all players. Figure out who holds the most cards, find out what they want the most and then offer to do exactly that.	Chapter 3
400	Déjà vu all over again.	Chapter 26
401	Revenge is not a dish to be eaten cold or hot—revenge is to be held close and nurtured and reviewed and studied and explored and embraced—and then to be taken internally, whether orally or by syringe, into a dark demon space and then used to create the fury of your own success.	Chapter 10
403	Use your opponent's power to keep returning the ball back to him.	Chapter 3
404	What seems like a problem is often nothing more than an opportunity looking to be found.	Chapter 3
407	When whistling and praying in the graveyard at the same time, try the tune from "Only the Good Die Young", Billy Joel	Chapter 25
408	Knowing the difference between RAM and ROM is nice, but a working knowledge of Shakespeare and Dylan can carry you a long way down the road.	Chapter 13
409	You have to do the somersault on the trapeze before you see the hands of your partner. If you wait to see him and then start your somersault you will fail and fall.	Chapter 30

RULE #	THE RULE	LOCATION
411	Try to enjoy the journey, because when you get there, the only thing left to do is check out.	Introduction, Chapter 14
412	Do not sweep the dogs under the rug—hang them on your wall right next to the moose head.	Chapter 14
431	Happily ever after. Hah!	Chapter 4
432	If you think yada yada is a substitute for rigorous thinking, you are about to lose your shirt.	Chapter 2
451	"Give me a long enough lever and a place to stand and I can move the world."—Archimedes	Chapter 4
452	When you hold the upper hand in a lopsided negotiation where you have 90% of the power, be very cautious to exercise it gently and to take care of the weaker party.	Chapter 3
453	Do not trust the appraiser or the rating agencies. An appraisal is an opinion of value, provided by someone who has no money in the deal, who gets paid long before the final scorecard is tallied. If he is wrong, he is usually not around to pick up any small pieces of sharded glass and you will probably be left holding various pieces of luggage. Think Moody's, Standard and Poor's, along with the guy who said we could sell these condominiums for $600 per square foot.	Chapter 9
491	A picture is worth a thousand words.	Chapter 12, 19

INDEX

ACKNOWLEDGMENTS

There is nothing like getting fired or failing miserably at your last job to inspire one to want to write a book.

First of all, you have time. You are lost and unemployed and licking your wounds and what better way to try to explain how the world should work instead of the way it does work than to write a book.

To that end, I need to thank a few of the people who made this adventure such a pleasure.

Dr. Gardner, my shrink of 18 years. We have reached a point in our work together where periodically we exchange chairs, and I sit and listen to him for an hour and say nothing. It gives him a chance to see how it feels to be in therapy. Then I send him a bill.

My children, Ethan and Rachel. They have inspired me to recall and relive all the sins of my own parents and to try desperately to avoid those, while at the same time seeking an opportunity to visit upon them new and different sins so they, too, will have a semi-miserable childhood and can later mine it as grist for their own mills.

My executive, worldwide, strategic, global administrative assistant, Ms. Nicole Rockstead. The word "assistant" does not do her justice. She has been with me for 18 years and knows every peccadillo, failing, quirk, flaw, and miserable behavior I have ever exhibited. And she has agreed to take these with her to her grave. She remembers the names of everyone I have ever worked with and we are in such simpatico that like a human Google keyword search engine, all I have to say is "do you remember, you know, what's his name, the guy with the red shirt . . ." and she has his name, email, and phone number on my desk in less than 30 seconds. She has performed every conceivable task from the most mundane (we spent three days and nights during the divorce trying to find the Visa bill from 1987) to the most difficult (the sale of every company and the details of every deal). She has a no-cut contract and is in the will—so don't even think of trying to steal her away.

Mr. Jeremy Cohen. We have been having coffee together since 1990, and I am extremely grateful for his advice and affection. Not only has he guided me through some very tough times, he has also taught me some basic Talmudic truths.

Mr. Danny Justman. He has abused me, picked on me, and made fun of me since 1974, and I am a better man for it. He too has a crusty exterior, but the soul of a saint. You just need a jackhammer to get through to the mohorovicic layer, and you are home free.

Lastly, and most importantly, my wife, Ms. Barbara Bry. People always say how they are eternally grateful. Well, I have put my money where my mouth and my heart are. You may remember the Curb Your Enthusiasm episode where Larry David hedges his affection by parsing the marital vow "'Til death do us part." Just in case there was something after death, he wanted to be free to explore. After all, he did life with Cheryl, but in the afterlife, he figured he ought to have a free shot at other goodies.

One of the great lines of romance comes from Paul Newman. When asked about his lifelong love with Joanne Woodward and the challenges of being a movie star, he remarked, "Why would I eat hamburger out when I have steak at home?"

I have vowed to my wife, not just "'Til death do us part," but rather I have signed up for eternity. The whole ballgame. The duration. Just in case there is another life coming up, I want to spend it with her.

Rule #84: When you have everything, don't keep reaching for anything else.

ABOUT THE AUTHOR

Neil Senturia has re-invented himself several times in his relentless pursuit of entrepreneurial success. Currently he is the CEO of Blackbird Ventures, an investor in high-growth potential companies and serves on several Boards of Directors.

Neil's diverse endeavors range from writing sitcoms to technology with a stint as a real estate developer in the middle. He has been CEO of six technology companies, three in software, one in material science, one in media, and most recently clean tech.

His companies have been sold to Cisco, Kofax, and Lockheed Martin. And no bio is complete without noting that one of the six went broke.

Neil has taught new venture creation as an adjunct professor in the MBA program at San Diego State University and has served on the Board of Directors of SDSU's Entrepreneurial Management Center. Currently he teaches entrepreneurship at UC San Diego's Jacobs School of Engineering von Liebig Center for Entrepreneurism and Technology Advancement. He is a member of the San Diego Venture Group and the MIT Enterprise Forum.

His numerous honors include winning the Microsoft Retail Application Developer Award twice, the Arnie Karush Award from the San Diego Software Industry Council, CONNECT's Most Innovative New Product Award, and CONNECT's lifetime contribution award in technology.

He is married to entrepreneur Barbara Bry, and their blended family includes four children between the ages of 25 and 29, and Momo, a Himalayan cat.